INVENTORY CONTROL

EASY

Nechelle Jones

authorHOUSE®

AuthorHouse™
1663 Liberty Drive
Bloomington, IN 47403
www.authorhouse.com
Phone: 1 (800) 839-8640

Published by AuthorHouse   01/19/2015

ISBN: 978-1-4969-6216-4 (sc)
ISBN: 978-1-4969-6215-7 (e)

CONTENTS

INTRODUCTION

This book was created in **Easy Form** for millions of people to have better knowledge and understanding of how to perform inventory and move forward toward a successful career. This book will teach you how to master, execute, and exceed inventory goals and budget goals. This book will increase your hourly wage or salary wage. You will learn some basic of accounting, finance, and the key process of inventory control. Maybe you have never worked for a company that has inventory but you have the potential and interested in learning more about the inventory field; maybe you are a manager who wants to improve your inventory; maybe you are a high school student and math is your favorite subject; or maybe you can't attend college due to different reasons, but you want a good promising career; etc. Whichever the reason this book is for you!! You will never have to work for minimum wage pay again! This will highly increase your knowledge, understanding, resume, career, and qualify you for 100's of jobs in different fields around the U.S. Mastering inventory tasks sounds hard, but it is fairly easy. Inventory is very important and a top priority too many companies and businesses around the world. Without inventory companies and businesses will have to close its doors.

I have been an Inventory and Financial Specialist for 25+ years, for National and International companies. Six years before becoming an Inventory Specialist, and Top Store Manager for numerous of regions and states, I wanted to become an Assistant Manager, Store Manager, Regional Trainer, District Manager, and Inventory Specialist. To accomplish these above goals I would work my 10 hours a day shifts weekly within the company and try when I could between my duties to take notes; train on the job; and seek advice from other Superior Managers in my store on how to work and execute all departments within the store in order to get promotions within the company. I quickly realized most companies **DO NOT** have enough tools and training hours to give most of their employees who want to be promoted within the company. They don't have a training program that will specifically train their employees and managers with patients on how to **MASTER, EXECUTE, AND EXCEED** Inventory, financial numbers, their position as managers, to exceed and execute all company goals, exceed payroll, exceed systems controls, exceed and execute operations, production, and keep a great team. The amount of revenue (money) it takes to train employees is a lot of the reason why many companies and businesses will not invest in this type of training for their employees. This is why I invested in myself and others to achieve the goal in mastering inventory within any company in easy form.

If companies and business would invest in this type of training program they would have even greater profit margins and increasing revenue throughout each year (Increasing Record Breaking Numbers). Most companies hire their employees and managers; then they train them for four days or two weeks on the job they were hired to do only. Most companies also give their employee's different test on chemical, health department rules, Serv Safe, manager's daily task, and the employee's daily job functions during their training process. These types of training from companies are good, but it's not Top Execution Training in Controlling Inventory to Exceed Company's Profit Margins. The majority of companies DO NOT have a training class that will only teach their employees how to master and execute cost of goods, budgeting payroll schedules, financial information, food cost, hourly rate target, cash flow, budgeting monthly and quarterly reports, gauging gross profits, audits, auditor, operation profits, keeping numbers in line, state & federal requirements, and other critical matters that effect inventory and the company's profit. If companies had this type of training program there would be more companies performing at Top Level Success each year. Most companies and business will inform their employees and managers of the company's budget goals and sales goals each month and for the year; but companies don't teach their employees and managers how to reach and exceed these budget goals and sales goals.

All of the above I had to master on my own time within six years with little help from co-workers and managers who didn't have time to train me and focus on their own daily job task. I worked each day on the job looking, learning, studying, and training for all positions and departments with the company. I spent countless hours after work in my home reviewing and mastering inventory and budgets for companies such as retail stores, fast food chains, restaurant, production plants, hotels, and etc. My goal was accomplished in 1991; I then became instantly a Company Trainer; four months later I became an Assistant Manager; five months later I became a Store Manager; One year later I became an Regional Manager; two years later I because an Inventory Specialist for multi-companies in different cities and states such as: Alabama, Florida, Mississippi, Atlanta, New Orleans, and throughout the Southeastern Region. During my 25+ years of working with multiple companies, I have increased the revenue of many National and International companies; and increased company's bottom line profit at 41% and more each year. I accomplished and over exceeded in building and restoring many companies by tracking and executing their inventory; and by training and working with employees and managers. I trained many management teams how to put a profitable inventory Action Plan together that will show increasing results in sales and revenue within six weeks; this includes improving the company's inventory counts, tracking inventory, ordering, building inventory, building a profitable team, troubleshooting, etc. I enjoyed using the tools in this book in training over 952 employees throughout the Southeastern Region to become Top Inventory Managers, Company Trainers, District Managers, Regional Manager, and most employees opened their own business. I am proud to say 96% of the employee's income has increased to over **$45,000 yearly, up to 6 figure digits yearly.** All the companies and employees who I have trained over the years are still growing today with great increasing sales, revenue, and profits.

This book will also help employees advance and achieve promotion goals, and increase your yearly income; and you will be able to increase a company's revenue as well. You will be able to execute inventory and all of the above I mentioned in this introduction. You will be able to start immediately on increasing your goals and increasing company goals and profits for **TOP LEVEL SUCCESS**.

PART 1

Let's Talk About the Inventory Career

A career in inventory is interesting each day and each day is never the same. An inventory person is similar to a detective. An Inventory career makes a job more motivating and enjoyable. Inventory allows you to monitor, challenge and improve your own career for successful results; this job is never boring. Inventory is a career for individuals with a strong sense of order who enjoy providing the kind of detailed support that will help the business run smoothly. The inventory person should like the idea of being a necessary part of the whole operation. An inventory person has a lot of tasks to complete each day, but they must always maintain calm, have patients and orderly profile in order to be very successful. They also enjoy analyzing the process of investigation, and establishing the facts, and developing and maintain a business. They are challenged by problem solving, increasing efficiency, and generally improving operations and production. They also enjoy working with people (people's person), but they are more interested in increasing productivity than in focusing on making friends. This is not to be seen a demeaning activity but as an honorable and satisfying one. When an inventory person is working a company; they are in charge and can gauge how highly successful their own career will be and how highly successful the company will be also. An inventory person and inventory is very important to most businesses.

An inventory person and a auditor do basically the same thing; they work in businesses of all kinds, check invoices, and accounting records for their accuracy. Among other tasks they make sure that payment have gone to the right persons and review all financial reports. An Inventory Manager combines mathematical, basic computer skills, manages with techniques, study all the business operations and suggest ways of solving any problems in the operation that they discover. Once the study is made, the manager prepares a written report (Action Plan) stating how they will improve inventory and how they will implement training employees to improve operations and production, revise company procedures, and monitor the affects of the new procedures they put in place. A inventory person always monitor the sales projections (the money goal the business wants to make within a time period) and the product in the business. They monitor the business current financial operating results and monitor the business current budget results. An Inventory person works in many kinds of retail stores, fast food stores, restaurants, wholesales stores, manufacturing and production companies, etc. They must obtain products or items of a specified quality at the lowest possible price. The products they buy range from raw materials for manufacturing companies, products from

1

wholesalers, and they also focus on office supplies, etc. They review and follow up on production schedules and check the quality of all products received. An inventory person is responsible for having the right amount of products on hand to make sure production and operations run smoothly. They make sure to buy products and supplies at competitive prices and place orders in accordance with sales trends and production schedules.

They are responsible for informing and posting any information about inventory results; good or bad. They make sure all products are categorized in the correct department. They are concerned with keeping track of missing products; tracking any false information concerning inventory; and tracking any inaccurate records. An inventory person monitors shipping and receiving of all products; and keep records of all materials transferred between the business and its sister stores, and their customers. They check all out going orders to make sure all the proper products are packed and the correct rate to make sure it is not too expensive. They check and process orders that arrive in the business. They make sure all orders are correct; they check for damage products, and then they send the order that they just received to their proper department within the business. An inventory person is always willing to learn more each day; the willing to be able to give instructions; able to work with little or no supervision; love to be competitive; they are risk takers; creative; people oriented; outdoor person and indoor person; like to communicate with others and don't mind physical work.

PART 2

KEYS TO THE FINANCIAL REPORT

8 KEY PEOPLE WHO COUNTS ON ACCURATE INVENTORY & FINANCIAL REPORTS

EXECUTIVE AND MANAGERS: They need accurate information; so they can know how well the company is performing. They also need to monitor the company's financial position; and look for problems that need to be improved; and see how well the company is doing in production. They need to troubleshoot any areas of improvement.

INVENTORY MANAGERS: They need to know the exact value of all the company's inventory and they must closely monitor the inventory at all times; so they can track the company's inventory. They must always value the company's inventory, and attract more sales, revenue, and profits for the company. They have a major impact on the company's financial reports.

EMPLOYEES: They need to know how well they're meeting or exceeding their company's goals and where they need to improve as well.

CREDITORS: They need to understand a company's financial position, to decide whether the company is meeting the requirement of any loans. They also decide whether to risk lending more money to a company.

INVESTORS: They need information to decide whether a company is a good investment. Investors like to invest in companies that are on a stable growing trend.

GOVERNMENT AGENCIES: These agencies need to be sure that all regulations set at the state and federal levels are in compliance by companies. These government agencies make sure that companies report their financial position accurately.

ANALYSTS: They need to review accurate information from a company for their clients who are considering the company for investments or additional loan funds.

FINANCIAL REPORTERS: They need to provide accurate information of a company's operations and report this information to the general public.

COMPETITORS: The Executive Staff will read the financial reports of its competitors'. They do this to see how their competitors are performing; so they can compete with their competitors. They will make decisions basic on their competitors such as: they will increase or decrease their prices on certain items or products; or they will start selling a product that the competitors sell.

1. **Financial Report** = Give a big picture of the value of a company at the end of a particular period. **Financial Health** = views a company's operations and whether it made profit.
2. **Financial Reporting Summary of A company's Numbers=**
    a. **ASSETS** = The cash, buildings, land, marketable securities, equipment, vehicles, copyrights, patents, tools and any other items needed to run a business that the company own.
    b. **COST AND EXPENSES**= The money spent to operate a business such as: payroll; compensation for employees; expense for production; supplies to run the business and offices; interior and exterior maintenance of the business building, and property, factories.
    c. **SALES** = Products or services that customers purchases from a business
    d. **LIABILITIES** = This is money that a company owes to outsiders such as loans, bonds, and unpaid bills, vendors, suppliers, contractors, employees, government, and etc.
    e. **PROFIT OR LOSS** = The amount of money a business or company earns or loses.
    f. **EQUITY** = Money that is invested in the company or business
    g. **CASH FLOW** = The amount of money that flows into and out of a business that is being reported during a specific time period.

DOUBLE-ENTRY ACCOUNTING = Shows both sides of every transaction in the company's books and those sides must be equal (must match). **EXAMPLE** = If a person spend $200.00 in cash on copy paper for the office. The value of the office supplies account increases by $200.00; and the value of the cash account will decrease by $200.00.

*NOTE: If a person buys a microwave two things will happen: **(1).** They will have something new. **(2).** They will have to give up cash, or use their credit card. A company that uses Double Entry Accounting will show both sides of these transactions in their books; and both sides should match.

SEC (SECURITIES AND EXCHANGE COMMISSION) = Only Public Companies that sells stock on the open market are required to reports to the SEC.

QUARTERLY REPORTS = Companies with holdings over $75 million must file a quarterly report; and it must be released within 45 days of the quarter's end.

ANNUAL REPORTS = Companies with over $75 million in assets must file their Annual Reports within 60 days. Small companies must file with 90 days of the end of their fiscal year.

FINANCIAL STATEMENTS = The majority of companies and business have reports called Balance Sheets / Income Statement / Statement of Cash Flows

BALANCE SHEET = Keeps track of a companies' financial balance. This sheet is a summary of the company's financial earnings or loss at a specific point in time. The following terms will typically appear on a balance sheet:

   a. **ASSETS** = Anything the company owns, from cash, to inventory, and the paper it prints the report on, to the vehicles it owns.
   b. **LIABILITIES** = Debts the company owes (money the company owes out)
   c. **EQUITY** = The value of property beyond the amount owed on it. Companies and business asset minus the liabilities. The company's owners will make claims such as shares of stock.

INCOME STATEMENT = This will tell management, cooperate executive, and other concerned people whether a company made a profit or took a loss. This will also give information about the company's revenues, its sales levels, how much money the company spent to make those sales and the expenses it paid to operate the business.

These are the key parts of the INCOME STATEMENT:

   a. **SALES OR REVENUES** = How much money the business took in from its sales from customers.
   b. **COST OF GOODS SOLD** = What it cost the company to produce or purchase the goods it sold.

c. **EXPENSES** = How much the company spent on rent, administration, advertising, salaries, and everything else it takes to operate a business to support the sales process.

d. **NET INCOME OR LOSS** = This is the bottom line that tells whether a company or business made profit or operated at a loss.

- **You can also expect to find the following 2 on the INCOME STATEMENT**

1. **EXCESS OF REVENUES OVER EXPENSES** = This report means the company earned a profit.

2. **EXCESS OF EXPENSES OVER REVENUES** = This report means the company faced a loss.

*Some people call the INCOME STATEMENT a **P & L (PROFIT AND LOSS)** = This is a summary report and statement of the company's operations. Summary statement of the company's earnings and summary statement of the company's operating results.

STATEMENT OF CASH FLOWS = Actual cash the company has available for continuing operations the next year; this is also called **CASH AND SHORT-TERM INVESTMENTS** at the end of year.

CASH EQUIVALENTS = Any holdings (assets) the company can easily change to cash. This includes cash, cash in checking and savings accounts, money-market funds, and stocks sold on the major exchanges that can be easily converted to cash, and certificates of deposit that are redeemable in less than 90 days.

CASH-BASIS ACCOUNTING = Tracks the actual cash going in and out of the business; it also tracks the amount of cash a company has available.

***Expenses & Revenues** = This has to be carefully matched on a month-to-month basis. If expenses and revenue aren't carefully match the company will not recognize all of its expenses until they actually pays the money; even if the company incurs the expenses in previous months.

TAX LIABILITY ACCOUNTING = An account for tracking tax payments that the company has made and must still make.

DOUBLE-ENTRY ACCOUNTING = EXAMPLE:

ACCOUNT	DEBIT	CREDIT
Office Supplies	+$200.00	
Cash		-$200.00

a. **DEBIT** = You will see this (debit) on the Double –Entry Accounting; this means increases in the value of Office Supplies Account. The company owns $200.00

in office supplies. This also means the company's assets grow because it now owns $200.00 worth of office supplies. Which is a (+)

   b. **CREDIT** = You will see this (credit) on the Double-Entry Accounting; this means decreases in the value of the cash account. The company had to spend $200.00 of its money to buy the office supplies. This also means the company no longer has $200.00 in the bank, because it was spent on office supplies. Which is a (-)

*BOTH ACCOUNTS ARE ASSET ACCOUNTS = This means both accounts represent things the company owns. Other asset that the company owns will also be shown on the Balance Sheet.

*PROFIT & LOSS = Shows a company's revenue and expenses over a set period of time. This will also show if the company operated at a profit or loss.

DEBITS & CREDITS ON SALE

ACCOUNT	DEBIT	CREDIT
Cash	+200.00	
Sales Revenue		+$200.00

In this case both Debit and Credit are **(+)**

Cash = The customer pays the company $200.00 for the company's product which is a (+) because the company now has $200.00 more in money. The Balance Sheet & Income Statement both keeps track of the amount of cash customers pay to buy the company's product.

Sales Revenue = The company's sales increased (+) by $200.00 when the customer pays for the product.

This is why both Debit and Credit accounts are a (+)

Companies and businesses have to make sure the Debits and Credits transactions are being recorded in the books correctly.

*In this case both the cash account & sales revenue account **increase.**

EXAMPLE: When debits & credits increase or decrease an account.

ACCOUNT	DEBIT	CREDITS
Assets	Increase	Decrease
Income	Decreas	Increase

Liabilities	Decrease	Increase
Expenses	Increase	Decrease

*Always review the Debit & Credit in each department that is assigned to you or company's accounts until you become familiar with the differences.

THE EFFECT OF DEBIT & CREDIT OF DEPRECIATION AND AMORTIZATION

EXAMPLE: When Debit & Credit both Increases

*When a company pays $45,000 for a car using a loan, it records the purchase this way:

ACCOUNT	DEBIT	CREDITS
2015 Jazzy's Company Car	$45,000	
Loan payable Vehicles		$45,000

*Debit & Credit Increases

Debit Increase= the total dollar amount of the assets (2015 new company car) this will be placed in the vehicle account

Credit Increase=due to the new loan, the total of loan payable will be $45,000 for the company new car

A company car has 5 years depreciation = This shows how old the car (assets) is and how much value and useful life the car or assets has.

* The 2015 Jazzy's company car is worth $45,000 divided by () 5 years depreciation = **$9,000**

The company records its depreciation expenses for the car at the end of each year this way:

ACCOUNT	DEBIT	CREDITS
Depreciation Expense	$9,000	
Accumulated Depreciation		$9,000

*In this case the Debit Increases the expenses for depreciation.

*Credit Increases the amount accumulated for depreciation.

CHART OF ACCOUNTS appears in the following order:

    a. Balance Sheet Assets Account = numbers usually are 1,000-1,999
    b. Liability Accounts = numbers usually are 2,000-2,999
    c. Equity Account = numbers usually are 3,000-3,999
    d. Income Statement Accounts / Revenue Accounts = numbers usually are 4,000-4,999
    e. Expense Accounts = numbers usually are 5,000-5,999

NOTE: Review your Company's Chart of Accounts until you become familiar with the company's number process.

TANGIBLE ASSETS = Assets that you can hold in your hand

1. **CURRENT ASSET** = Assets that the company owns and will use up in the next 12 months. **Inventory** and **Accounts Receivable** are also current assets.

Example: Cash in checking, cash in savings, cash on hand, accounts receivable, and Inventory.

2. **LONG-TERM ASSETS** = Assets that a company will hold for more than 12 months:

Example: Land, buildings, equipment, furniture and fixture, molds, tools, dies accumulated depreciation, leasehold improvements, and vehicles.

CAPITALIZED LEASES = When a company takes ownership of a contract such as a building by using a lease agreement. The lease agreement that the company holds will give the company the option to purchase that property at some point in the future. A person can also find this on the Balance Sheet.

LEASEHOLD IMPROVEMENTS = Companies track improvements to property they lease and don't own. These items are depreciated because the improvements will most likely lose value as it age. A person can also find this on the Balance Sheet.

MACHINERY AND EQUIPMENT = Companies track, summarize, and record all machinery and equipment used in their facilities or by their employees. The machinery and equipment depreciate the same as building and vehicles; but machinery and equipment last for a shorter period of time. A person can find this on the Balance Sheet.

FURNITURE AND FIXTURES = Mostly Retail Outlets will have a separate line for furniture and fixtures on their financial sheet. Retail Outlets will have this line on the Balance Sheet. Other companies will most likely have furniture and fixtures items included in machinery and equipment or other assets.

TOOLS, DIES, AND MOLDS = Companies that manufacture their own products will have tools, dies, and molds on the balance sheet. Businesses that don't manufacture their own products will not put this on the balance sheet. Tools, dies, and molds can have significant value if they are unique and are developed specifically by or for a company. The value of tools, dies, and molds will depreciate in time as well. **Example:** If a company's manufacturing department makes cups with "Let's party in 2015" imprinted on them; in 2016 these cups will lose value because the year 2015 imprinted on the cups has passed.

INTTELLECTUAL PROPERTY= Copyrights, trademarks, and patents, written work, products that are registered with the government. The government grants patents (exclusive rights) to individuals or companies that invents a new product or process.

GOODWILL = This is when a company has bought another company. A company will purchase and pay more for the business than the business is actually worth. The company will not take on any of the business liabilities when it buys the business.

LIABILITY ACCOUNTS

A. **CURRENT LIABILITY ACCOUNTS** = Money owed in the next 12 months.

Example: Accounts Payable, Sales Tax Collected, Accrued Payroll Taxes, Credit Card Payable, etc.

B. **LONG-TERM LIABILITY** = Money due beyond the next 12 months.

Example:

(1) **Loans Payable** = Such as mortgages, loans on vehicles, that a company will have to make payments on longer than one year.
(2) **Bonds payable** = Corporate bonds that have been issued for the term longer than one year. Bonds are a type of debt sold on the market that must be repaid in full with interest.

PRIVATE COMPANIES = Private companies don't have to report to the public or the government. Of course they do have to file their tax return each year. Private companies don't sell stock to the general public.

*Private companies give owners the freedom to make their own choices within the company without having to consult with outside investors' opinions.

* No matter how big or small a private company is they can operate behind closed doors.

*Private companies control their own pay and employees payroll; and they make their decisions based on their own preferences.

*Private companies must file financial report with SEC when it has more than 500 common shareholders such as (Executives, Managers, Creditors, and Investors), and $10 million in assets.

PUBLIC COMPANIES

PUBLIC COMPANIES = Offers **Shares** and **Stock** on the open market.

Public Company Owners = Don't make decisions based on their own preferences, because they must always consider the opinions of the business's outside investors.

*Public Companies = Must generate $10 million to $20 million in annual sales, with profits of about $1 million.

*Public Companies = Must file **Quarterly Audited Financial Statements** on **Form 10 Q**. Public companies that have market risks, legal proceeding, defaults on payments, and controls and procedures must report this information as well on the Form 10Q.

*Public Companies Yearly Report** = Must file an annual report with financial statements and information about the following:

A. **Company History** = How the company was started, who started it, and how it grew to its current level of operation.
B. **Organizational Structure** = How the company is organized, who the key executives are, and who reports to whom.
C. **Equity Holdings** = A list of all their major shareholders and summary of all the company's outstanding stock
D. **Subsidiaries** = This is other business that the company owns or partially owns.
E. **Employee Stock Purchase and Savings Plan** = These are Plans that allow employees to own stock by purchasing it or allows employees to participate in a savings plan.
F. **Incorporation** = This gives information about the location and where the company is incorporated.
G. **Legal Proceedings** = This gives information about any ongoing, or upcoming legal matters that the company may be facing.
H. **Changes or Disagreements With Accountants** = Information about financial disclosures, control and procedures, executive compensation, and accounting fees and services.

*Public Companies = Must file a **Form 8-K** to report any major events that can impact the company's financial position. Critical events that should be reported on a Form 8K such as: the sale of a company division or company; bankruptcy; resignation of directors; business combination; financial results; disposal assets; accountant change, temporary suspension of employee benefit; change in laws and charter; amendments to company's code of ethic, change in fiscal year.

Form 8-K = A form that must be filed by companies if they have any major changes within the company; this must be reported on an 8-K Form to the SEC within 4 days of the event.

Sarbanes – Oxley Act = Requires the signature of the CEO's and CFO's. This will certify that the CEO's and CFO's have read and approved the financial and other information contained in their Quarterly & Annual Reports.

GAAP (Generally Accepted Accounting Principles)= Guidelines a auditor follow to make sure that company's financial statements are presented fairly and accurate. This helps the company decide and measure the amount of financial information to report such as: assets, liabilities, equity, expenses, revenue, etc.

PART 3

ANNUAL REPORT

Annual Report = This is also called the Financial Statement. The Financial Statement is **NO DOUBT** the meat of an annual report; there are many reports and statements that make up an annual report.

Four (4) Keys You Need to Focus On In An Annual Report:

1. **Auditors' Report** = A statement by the auditors regarding the findings of their audit of the company's financial books.
2. **Financial Statement** = The Balance Sheet, Income Statement, and Statement of Cash Flows.
3. **Note to the Financial Statement** = Additional need to know information that is on the financial statement. This information could be great news for the company's financial position or critical news for the company's financial position.
4. **Management's Discussion and Analysis (MD&A)** = Management's perspective regarding the company's bottom line results. The management's statement will give juicy information about the company's positive and negative situations and problems that impacted the company's financial position. This report will tell how smoothly the company was running all year or what when wrong. This report will give an idea of how well a company will perform and operate in the future as well.
5. **A letter to the shareholders** from the CEO and the Chairman Board will be on the front of most Annual Reports. This letter will highlight the company's growing increasing profits and how great the company did in that year. The negative result will most likely be hidden in the middle of the letter; sometimes the company will not even mention any negative results.

*These are Key words for hidden trouble inside a company or business.

    A. **Challenging** = When a company is facing significant difficulties selling its product or service.
    B. **Restructuring** = When the companies task or action plan is not working or something within their operation isn't working

C. **Corrective Actions are Being Taken** = This will be in the notes on the financial statements or the management's discussion & analysis about poor performance that has been documented.

D. **Difficulties** = The difficulties the company or business faced during the fiscal year will be in the management's discussion & analysis (MD&A), or the financial statements.

(SEC) = Monitors the MD&A section closely to make sure that companies present all critical information about current operations, capital, and liquidity. The SEC pays special attention to a number of key factors that the MD&A is supposed to cover: (such as)

A. **Revenue Recognition** = Recognizing revenue can be very tricky, because many times the purchase includes multiple parts. This means when a customer has to buy two or more things to make one particular item work such as: The customer can buy an printer, scan, and copy machine, but they will have to separately buy the ink to operate this machine; and many times they will have to separately buy the cable connecters for the machine as well; so recognizing the revenue for each of these items can vary.

B. **Impairments To Assets** = Companies must immediately report assets that are damaged or destroyed, losses of assets, and any lost in a company's value to their shareholders in a timely manner.

C. **Pension Plans** = This is an account for pension plans that gives important information about the amount the company will pay out when employees retire. The pension plans also tracks the amount of interest or other gains the company expect to make on their assets they hold in their pension plan.

D. **Environmental and Product Liabilities** = Products that fail to operate as expected or products that cause damage to an individual or property will be the responsibility and liability of the company. All companies face some liability for their products that fail. This includes some industries that sells and produce oil, chemicals, gas, etc.

A. **Stock-Based Compensation** = Some Top Executives get stock based compensation as part of their payroll. Many companies offer stock incentives that include shares of stock as bonuses as part of an employee compensation package.

B. **Allowance For Doubtful Accounts** = Companies that offers credit to customers will most likely have problems with some non-paying customers. You will also see this in the company's **Customers Pass Due Account File**. If you are working in a company that offers credit to customers carefully review the customers pass due account. Non-paying customers will impact the company's bottom line. The company will lose big profit and sometimes plenty of their assets.

MD&A = This report will explain any major competitions, inflation, interest expenses, and other issues that may impact the company's future success. This report will also have the following information

A. Discussion about whether the company sales increased or decreased.
B. Details on how well the company performed in their production line and the quality of their product.
C. An explanation of the company's economic situation that may have impacted the company's performance and sales.
D. **Distribution Systems=** This describes how the company's products are being distributed.
E. **Product Improvements =** The company will explain the changes that were made to its products that improved their performance or appearance.
F. **Manufacturing Capacity =** This is the number of the company's manufacturing plants and their manufacturing production capability.
G. **Research and Development Projects =** Many companies and businesses develop their own products. These types of companies also develop new products as well. Many companies must have research and development for new products or to improve their current products.
H. **Cost-Control Problems =** When a company purchase raw materials the cost of the raw materials many times will not stay the same. This is when the price of the raw materials will increase and decrease often. (Isn't Stable)

Capital Resources = This will show the company's assets; and will show if a company has the ability to fund its operations for a long term. Capital Resources will show if the company is in a strong financial position.

Liquidity = A company's cash position and its ability to pay its bills for a short-term or on a day-to-day basis.

Auditors' Report = This report will show if the auditor raised any Red Flags about the company's Financial Statement. The auditor will not give any information about whether a company is a good investment. The auditor will not give out information about a company's financial position.

The Auditor's Report has 3 keys

A. **Introductory Paragraph =** This will show the time period the auditor reviewed and covered the company's financial reports. It will also show the manager or executive member who is responsible for the financial statements.
A. **Scope Paragraph =** This is the paragraph in which the auditors will make statements that the company's financial statement is free from misstatement and free from misleading information. The auditor will also state that they planned and performed the audit by using acceptable audit standards.

***Material Misstatements =** This is when a company makes an mistake that can significantly impact the company's financial position. Some companies will report revenue before they actually earned the revenue.

***Misleading information =** When a company will make false statements or produce false numbers involving their bottom line numbers. When a company makes false reports on the financial statement concerning the company's financial position in order to make the company's revenue look stronger and better.

C. Opinion Paragraph = The auditors states their opinion of the company's financial statements. If the auditors don't find any problems with the financial statements, the auditor will simply state that the statements in the financial statements are prepared with generally accepted accounting principles "(GAAP).

Non Standard Auditors' Report = This is when an auditor find a problem in the company's financial statement. The auditor will explain their opinions and notes problems areas that they found in the company's financial statement.

Example:

A. **Work Performed By A Different Auditor**= When a company has a different auditor than it had in previous years. When a company changes auditors this issue should be researched and investigated. The company should explain in great detail the reason why the company changed auditors. When a company changes auditors this should raise a red flag for many questions.

B. **Accounting Policy Changes** = If a company change its accounting policies or change its accounting procedures the auditor must note the change in a non standard auditors' report. These changes may not indicate that the company has a problem. The auditors may agree that the company had a good reason for making the change to its accounting policies or accounting procedures. If the auditor disagrees with company's change the auditor will state their opinion in the non-standard auditor report.

MATERIAL UNCERTAINTIES = When an auditor finds an area in the financial statement that raise serious questions concerning the company's potential financial position. The auditor may find financial consequences that the company may face such as: pending lawsuits that maybe damaging to the company's financial position if it loses the lawsuit, agreement violations, loss of a major customer, etc. The company's management staff and the auditor will have to estimate and determine what it will cost the company financially if the company loses the pending issues.

Going-Concern Problems = If the auditor have doubt that a company has the ability to stay in business, they will indicate that the company has a going-concern problem. (Capital Deficiencies or Significant Contract Dispute)

Specific Disclosures = The Auditor will make note and explain situations about the company that they believes the public needs to know. These are situations that are not a serious problem.

Qualified Opinions = This is an auditors final paragraph of the report. This paragraph will also state when an auditor finds an issue in the company's financial statement that raised concerns; but the auditor didn't have the proper information available during the audit to determine whether this issue will have an impact on the company financial position.

BALANCE SHEET

THE ACCOUNT FORMAT

BALANCE SHEET = A balance sheet has 3 different styles:

      A. **Account Format**
      B. **Report Format**
      C. **Financial Position Format**

Account Format = This presents the numbers in a horizontal style

Example:

Current Asset	$500	**Current Liabilities**	$400
Long-Term Asset	$250	**Long-Term Liabilities**	$300
Other Asset	$70	**Total Liabilities**	$700
Total Asset	$820	**Shareholder Equity**	$120
		Total Liabilities/Equity	$820

*A balance sheet shows a company's total assets which equals the company's total liabilities/equity

REPORT FORMAT = This presents the numbers in a vertical style

Example:

Current Assets	$500
Long-Term Assets	$250
Other Assets	$ 70
Total Asset	$820
Current Liabilities	$400
Long-Term Liabilities	$300
Total Liabilities	$700
Shareholders' Equity	$120
Total Liabilities/Equity	$820

FINANCIAL POSITION FORMAT = A financial position format is rarely use in companies in the United States. This format is mostly used internationally.

*Financial Position Format has additional lines that don't appear on the other two formats (Working Capital, Net Assets, Non-Current Assets)

> *A. **Working Capital** = Current assets the company has available to pay bills.
> *You find the working capital by subtracting the current assets from the current liabilities.
>
> *B. **Net Assets** = Shows what's left for the company's owners after all liabilities have been subtracted from total assets.
> *C. **Non-Current Assets** = Are long-term assets as well as assets that aren't current; but also aren't long-term, (Such as stock ownership in another company).

Example:

Current Asset	**$500**
Less: Current Liabilities	**-$400**
Working Capital	**$100**
Plus: Non-Current liabilities	**$600**
Total Assets Less	
Current Liabilities	**$700**
Less: Long-Term liabilities	**$200**
Net Assets	**$500**

FINANCIAL POSITION FORMAT = This format is also used when investing global (All over the world). This format is used when buying stock directly in European or other foreign companies.

*Companies that own other companies that are operating in another country use this format. Companies that are based in another country use this format.

*The company must keep the books according to U.S generally accepted accounting principles (GAAP) rules, and must meet the standards of the International Financial Reporting Standards (IFRS).

*Companies that operate in more than one country have a larger problem than the companies that operate in only one country. Companies that operate in more than one country must report financial position results to each country in which they operate, including the country in which the company is based.

*Cash, of course, is the important part of the balance sheet.

CASH = The cash is the most important part of the balance sheet. The most complicated task a company has is keeping track of the money. Some companies keep cash in many different locations; so keeping track of the money in multiple locations can be a difficult task.

*Companies must have a way of tracking it **cash** and knowing exactly how much it has at the end of each day. Most companies track their cash several times a day. Companies that have high-volume (very busy) stores will most likely track their cash several times a day.

*The person tracking and counting out the cash draw must show the cash amount matches up with the total day's transaction report. The transaction report indicates the amount of cash that should be in the cash draw.

*All company's locations need a bank to deposit receipts and get cash the company needs to operate the business daily. Each location that the company has calculates the cash total and reports this total to the assign accounting area within the company.

*The amount of cash that is on the balance sheet is the total cash amount of all the company's locations on the day in which the balance sheet was created by the company's accountant.

*Managing cash is one of the hardest jobs for companies and businesses, because cash can easily disappear if the proper money procedures aren't in place within the company.

Companies and businesses must have consistency in following all money procedures properly this includes making sure that all daily cash registers balance, petty cash balance, bank deposits balance, bank accounts balance, deposit log balance & signed daily by at least two people (the person who prepared the deposit & a witness who also verified the deposit), and daily transactions balance.

CURRENT LIABILITIES

SHORT-TERM BORROWINGS = This is when a company borrows credit to help with the cash issues. Sometimes companies will borrow cash from banks, investors, etc. in order to pay its bills. These types of short-term borrowing loans usually have high interest rates. If a company can't pay the loan quickly the loan will turn into long-term debt. Long –term has lower interest rates.

*Short-Term Borrowings liability should be a low number on the balance sheet, compared with other liabilities. A number that isn't low may be a sign that the company may be in trouble. This could mean the company is having problems paying its long-term debt.

CURRENT PORTION OF LONG-TERM DEBT = This will show all the company's payments that are due on long-term debt during the current fiscal year.

*(a). ACCOUNTS PAYABLE= This is a list that a company keep regarding the money they owe to others for supplies, products, and services. These are Invoices that a company must pay in less than 12 months.

*(b). ACCRUED LIABILITIES = This is liabilities that a company has accumulated within a time period, but the company hasn't paid for the liabilities at the time its accountant prepared the balance sheet such as: employee taxes, employee's payroll, income taxes, advertising expenses, etc.

This section will review some of a company's stock and the shareholders of stock, because they are also an important part of most company's inventory.

(STOCK)

*1. **STOCK**= Each share of stock has a certain value; this is based on the price placed on the stock when it was first sold to investors. When the stock market gains or losses its value this will actually impact the shareholders, not the company.

*2. **COMMON STOCK** = When shareholders own a portion of the company and they also have a vote on any of the company's issues and some of the companies decisions.

*3. **PREFERRED STOCK** = Shareholders that own stock in a company; this stock is between common stock and a bond. This is actually a long-term liability that the company will pay back over a number of years. Many companies pay these shareholders a certain amount each year. These shareholders don't have any voting rights in the company.

*4. **TREASURY STOCK** = This stock can be found on the financial report in the equity section on the balance sheet. This is stock that the company has bought back from shareholders. When a company buys back stock, this means that the company has fewer shares on the market. When a company has fewer shares, this tends to make the shares stock prices raise.

* When a company files bankrupt, the bondholders has first claim on any money remaining after the company pays the employees and other secured debtors (secured debtors are the people who've loaned money based on specific assets, such as a mortgage on a building).

CAPITAL = Small companies that are not publicly owned will most likely use capital on its balance sheet. If a company's owner didn't invest their own capital to start the business the balance sheet will not have a section for capital.

DRAWING ACCOUNT = This is the section that tracks any money that the owner takes out of the company's annually profits. This is used in unincorporated businesses.

PART 4

INCOME STATEMENT

INCOME STATEMENTS = This is a statement that reports the results of the company's operating period monthly and yearly. At the top of an income statement you will most likely see the phrase **"Year Ended" or "Fiscal Year Ended"** and the month the period ended for an annual financial statement. You may also see on an income statement the phrase **"Quarters Ended" or "Months Ended"** this reports is based on shorter periods of time.

*Companies are required to show at least 3 periods of the company's reports and operating results on their income statements, this means that if you're looking at an income statement for 2015, you will also find columns for 2014 and 2013.

MULTI-STEP FORMAT HAS (4) DIFFERENT PROFIT LINES:

*1.   **GROSS PROFIT =** This line will show you the profits that the company generated from its sales minus the actual cost of the goods sold.

*2.   **INCOME FROM OPERATIONS =** This line will show you the operating income the company earned after subtracting all its operating expenses.

*3.   **INCOME BEFORE TAXES =** This line will show you all the company's income they earned before the company subtract its taxes. This can include money the company earned from selling its equipment, interest revenue, etc.

*4.   **NET INCOME (OR) NET LOSS =** This line will show you the money the company earned on its bottom line. This will also show you whether the company made a profit or if the company had a loss.

COMPANY'S THAT SOMETIMES HAS TO ADJUST ITS SALES PRICES

ADJUSTING SALES

*1.   Companies don't always sell their products at their list price. Companies frequently use discounts, returns, and other methods to reduce the prices of its products or services.

Whenever a company sells a product at a discount, the company needs to keep track of all discounts and any returns. It's the only way the company can review how much money it's making on the sale of its products; and how accurately the company is pricing the products.

*2. When a company offers too many discounts within its business, it's usually a sign that the company may be in a weak or very competitive market. If a company has a lot of returns, it may be a sign of a quality-control problem. It could also be a sign that the product isn't living up to customers' expectations.

*3. The most common types of sales adjustment that companies makes are:

*a. **VOLUME DISCOUNTS** = When the company wants to get more items in the store. This is when the retailers agree to buy a large number of a manufacturer's product so they can save a certain percentage of money off the original price. This can also reduce a company's revenue.

*b. **RETURNS** = Arrangements between the buyer (customer) and seller (business) that allow the buyer to return goods for a lot of different reasons. Customers will return a product if it didn't work when they tried to use it; or the product didn't fit; or they didn't like the product. Returns are subtracted from a company's revenue and it can impact the company's sales.

*c. **ALLOWANCES** = Accounts that a customer pays for up front without taking the product. Allowances are actually liabilities for a business, because many customers will pay a little down on products and the business will take these products off their shelves for the customer until the customer comes back pay the remaining balance.

Then sometimes the customer never comes back; so the business now lost sales on these products that it took off the shelves for the customer. Many times these products will be off the shelves for days or weeks.

COST OF GOODS SOLD

COST OF GOODS SOLD = This is what it costs for a business to manufacture or purchase the goods being sold. The Cost of Goods is closely monitored by the companies Managers and the owner.

*Some items that make up the cost of goods sold will vary depending on whether a company manufactures the goods in-house (within the company) or purchases them. If a company manufactures the goods in-house, it will track the cost of the goods starting with the cost of the raw materials; and the company will include the labor involved in building the product. If the company purchases it goods, it tracks the purchases of the goods.

*A **Manufacturing company** tracks several levels of their **INVENTORY**, including:

A. **RAW MATERIAL** = The materials used for manufacturing
B. **WORK-IN-PROCESS INVENTORY** = Products in the process of being produced
C. **FINISHED-GOODS INVENTORY** = Products ready for sale

*These manufacturing companies also add any other costs such as: Freight Charges, and other cost that are involved with the goods being sold.

*Managing costs during the production process is critical for all manufacturing companies. During the production process managers need to make sure they monitor the correct cost it takes to produce the product. Manager must also monitor price hikes during the production stage. Managers in this type of business receive regular reports that include the cost detail. This report will show the managers if there is an increase in cost. If there's an increase in cost the managers must investigate this as quickly as possible. If the increase is not investigated quickly by the managers this will drastically impact the company's profit and revenue.

MONITORING GROSS PROFIT

GROSS PROFIT = This is the net revenue or net sales minus the cost of goods sold. This number shows the difference between what a company pays for its inventory and the price at which it sells this inventory. A Gross Profit number also tells you how much profit the company makes selling its products before deducting the expenses of its operation. CEO's, CFO, managers, investors, and other interested parties closely watch the company's gross profit because it indicates the effectiveness of the company's purchasing and pricing policies.

*If a company's profit is too low, a company can do one of two things:

- A. Find a way to increase sales revenue
- B. Find a way to reduce the cost of the goods it's selling

*To increase sales revenue, the company can raise or lower prices to increase the amount of money it's bringing in. Raising the prices of its product brings in more revenue if the same number of items is sold, but it may bring in less revenue if the prices are too high. If the prices are too high the customers will not buy the products and the company will sell fewer items.

EXAMPLE:

*(a) If a company sells 30 pencils in one week at .40 cents each, but the company raised the pencils price to .65 cents each. When the company raised the price of the pencils to .65 cents each, the company still sold 30 pencils in one week. This means that raising the price on the pencils will bring more revenue to the company.

EXAMPLE:

*(b) If a company sells 30 pencils in one week at .40 cents each, but the company raised the pencils price to .65 cents each. When the company raised the price of the pencils to .65 cents each, the company only sold 6 pencils in one week.

This means that raising the price on the pencils will bring less revenue to the company, because fewer pencils are sold.

Cost Control = When managers monitor the cost of all goods sold. *Manager should make sure that they are monitoring cost-control for all products that are received or delivered to the company. A manager should also make sure that all products that are received or delivered is really all there and in good condition.

PART 5

COMPANY'S EXPENSES

EXPENSES = A company have different types of expenses, which Include the items a company must pay for to operate the business that aren't directly related to the sale and production of specific products. A company has expenses, which includes the cost of the product it sales.

*Even when a company is making a sizable gross profit, if management doesn't carefully watch the expenses, the gross profit can quickly turn into a net loss.

*Advertising and Promotion, administration, and research and development are all examples of expenses.

ADVERTISING AND PROMOTION = Advertising includes TV and radio ads, print ads, and billboard ads. Promotions include product give away such as T-Shirts, hats, pens & cups with company logo printed on the cups. Advertising and promotions are large expenses for a company.

OTHER SELLING ADMINISTRATION EXPENSES = This category is for all the companies that has selling expenses that includes Sales People's, Sales Manager's Salaries, Bonuses, Commissions, and other compensation expenses.

OTHER OPERATING EXPENSES = This is all the company's operating expenses that aren't connected to the sale of its products.

    *A. GENERAL OFFICE NEEDS = Expenses that are needed in order for the company to run its operation. This is the company's expenses for its administrative office, supplies, machinery, human resources, management, security, etc.

*B.   ROYALTIES = When payments are made to individuals or companies to use its property.

*Some examples of royalties are the use of patents or copyright that another company or individual owns.

ACCOUNTS RECEIVABLE

ACCOUNTS RECEIVABLE = Are customers that can buy a product from the company on credit. The company has an accounts receivable line on its balance sheet. Customer has between 10 to 30 days from the billing date to pay their bill.

*Accounts receivable also list the money that customers owe the company for products or services they already received.

*A company must carefully monitor whether a customer pays their bills; and how quickly the customer pays their bills. If a customer constantly makes payments late, the company must determine whether to allow the customer to get additional credit or block the customer from any further purchases. A non-paying customer will hurt the company. Too many non-paying or late paying customers can drastically hurt a company's cash flow (revenue) to the point where the company is not able to pay its own bills.

*When Accounts Receivable increase during the year, this means the company sells more products or services on credit than it collects in actual cash from customers.

*If a company has a decrease in accounts receivable during the year, this means that the company collected more cash, and gave less credit to its customers during the year.

ACCOUNTS PAYABLE =This is when a company pays the bills that it owes. When a company's accounts payable increase, a company uses less cash to pay bills. The company will then have more cash on hand.

*This will make the company look like it has more cash on hand; but actually the company hasn't paid out the cash to pay its bills (expenses).

*If a company's accounts payable decrease, the company pays out more cash to pay its bills. A decrease in accounts payable means the company has less cash on hand.

INVESTMENT ACTIVITIES SECTION

INVESTMENT ACTIVITIES SECTION = This section can be found in the Cash Flow Statement. This will look at what the company purchase and the sale of any new assets such as:

    A. Upgrades to existing factories and equipment
    B. Purchases of new building, land, etc.
    C. Two companies that decides to mergers (join) together
    D. Purchases of new stocks or bonds

* A company can invest in upgrading its facility if a company is making this choice to grow and improve its business and profits.

*If the company is using most of its cash to keep old factories operating as long as possible, this could drain a company's revenue; and the company could loss profits.

CALCULATING ACCOUNTS RECEIVABLE TURNOVER

(1) **STEP FORMULA FOR TESTING ACCOUNTS RECEIVABLE TURNOVER:**
A. Calculate the average accounts receivable
B. Find the accounts receivable turnover ratio

*Net Sales + Average Accounts Receivable = Accounts receivable turnover ratio

*Find the average sales credit period (the time it takes customers to pay their bills):

*52 Weeks () divided by Accounts receivable turnover ratio = Average Sales Credit Period.

*It will be best to use annual credit sales instead of net sales for calculating accounts receivable turnover (only people who work within the company has access to the annual credit sales), because net sales include both cash and credit sales.

*People who are reading the financial statement, but they work outside the company (Auditor's) usually have to use the net sales. An outside person usually can't the out the credit sales numbers by reading the financial statement.

* Accounts Receivable Turnover by using <u>Income Statements & Balance Sheets.</u>

CALCULATING THE AVERAGE ACCOUNTS RECEIVABLE: 2014

A. (1,130,700,000 + 1,140,140,000) = 2,270,840,000
Income Statement Balance Sheet Average Account Rec.

B. 2,270,840,000 Divided by() 2 = 1,135,420,000
Average Account Receivable Averg. Account Rec.

CALCULATING ACCOUNTS RECEIVABLE TURNOVER RATIO

(Net Sales) = 4,245,682,000 Divided by () 1,135,420,000 = 3.74 times

Net Sales Averg. Account Rec.

CALCULATING THE AVERAGE SALES CREDIT PERIOD

52 Weeks (Divided by) () 3.74 (Accounts Receivable turnover ratio) = 13.90 Weeks.

*If your 2013 Average Sales Credit Period was 11.42 Weeks to collect from its customers, the company experienced a decline in its accounts receivable collection in 2014. This means that the company collected much faster from its customers in 2013 than it did in 2014.

ACCOUNTS RECEIVABLE AGING SCHEDULE = This report will show customers who have over due accounts; and the amount they owe the company; and the number of days their account is pass due.

Example:

Customer	35-45 Days	46-60 Days	61-90 Days	Over 90 Days	Total
Mike	$50	$50	$0	$0	$100
Lavette	$150	$100	$0	$50	$300
Sam	$50	$0	$0	$50	$100
Rita	$400	$250	$150	$100	$900
Total	$650	$400	$150	$200	$1,400

*Rita is the customer who owes the highest amount to the company.

*Lavette is the customer that owes the next highest amount to the company.

FIRST STEPS TO INVENTORY

THE FIRST STEPS TO INVENTORY

You have been reading, reviewing, and getting an understanding to other parts of operating a business such as: Financial Reports, Assets, Account Receivable, Account Payable, Stock, etc. Understanding all of the above will have successful result in your inventory.

Inventory is the meat and potatoes of many companies. Inventory is the most important part to keeping a business in operation. Inventory management must always keep track of inventory. Failure to keep track of a company's inventory is basically the same as guaranteeing failure of the business.

The Inventory Manager is the key to running a successful business. A good Inventory Manager will make a company see an increase in its sales and profit.

It is very important for all the company's inventory to be categorized.

Example: Dairy, Accessories, Electronics, Produce, Books, Furniture, Apparel, Shoes, Wares (pots, plates, cups, etc.), Pharmacy, etc.

Inventory must always have an accurate beginning and ending count of all the company's products within a location, in order to get accurate figures and results at the end of each accounting period.

Inventory should have a template (Par-Level) that shows the company's product history of usages and sales trends. In this section you will review Par Levels.

Inventory in most businesses has a computerized system that automatically has a tracking ability to update when items are received and sold within the business.

Inventory tracking is useful not only just for knowing how much stock a business have on hand or how much product was sold, but also to have accurate accounting for the company's tax purpose.

Most company's count their inventory weekly, monthly, and sometimes yearly. Most companies that counts their inventory once a year; tends to have more trouble tracking its inventory; tends to over order products from vendors throughout the year; finds more mistakes on invoices that are too late to correct and is subject to more theft problems.

Inventory is a mayor balance between sales, customers, available products, production and seasonal demands.

An Inventory Manager allows the reordering of products and they should know how much product to purchase. To achieve this, the Inventory Manager must put together several different action plans to make sure inventory is successful and profitable. Inventory starts with your initial beginning count. Maybe you're counting your inventory levels for the first time, or perhaps you don't trust your current numbers and you want to start a "new clean count". Whichever the reason for your inventory count, make sure you get a complete and accurate count of all the product levels. This will give you a trusted number and a good picture of your current inventory levels.

*Key decisions to make before conducting your inventory count:

(a). Why are you counting your inventory?

Businesses already have a good reason for counting inventory. This is a good time to consider other benefits to keeping track of inventory and the reasons for tracking inventory. Manager's who count the company's inventory should often remind themselves the reason for tracking inventory, as well as to stimulate their imagination as to why they count and track inventory.

Asset tracking and valuation are also a large part of inventory; due to most businesses have a large part of their capital tied up in assets. You can't get the best use of your assets if you only have a small idea of what they are.

(b). What are you going to count?

Counting and managing stock levels can avoid over ordering of certain items. This will free up space for new products. Most businesses or companies that have product stock demand changes to their inventory based on the seasons, such as: holidays, local events, time of year, etc; the business must have an accurate count of items or products that are most affected by these factors. The business should know how much of an item or product that was used last time, and how much was left over so they can decide how much to order this time, this is also called a **Par-Level**.

Inventory counts also help to avoid **shrinkage, theft**, and **loss control**.

If people know that no one's keeping track of items and products, they will start to become careless at the most; and also outright theft will start at the worst. When a business controls and performs its inventory counts, this shows people that counting of its goods and equipment is a regular part of their operations, because they care about their profit. People and employees will know that the company and its management team are paying close attention, and they will also start paying close attention as well.

Most businesses set up their storage locations by feel, or sometimes by a habit. Once you practice tracking inventory you may make a better decision on the best and safe location for your products.

Inventory is very important in a case of a disaster strike. Inventory tracking depends on how quickly a business will be able to account for all the product and equipment that was lost. Ask yourself "What if all your inventory value was gone tomorrow"? Having the current and accurate inventory count and value would be great for the businesses and their insurance company. It will be much easier for the business to give their insurance carrier an accurate count of what items were lost and damaged in a disaster.

Each ending inventory count is always reported and sent to the accounting department, also at the end of every fiscal year. A solid record of inventory can make an annual report a much easier task to complete.

(c). Where are you going to count?

Always count the location where items may exist that needs to be counted. Some businesses have one or two locations to count, and others have thousands of locations to count. An Inventory Manager needs to make sure everyone knows which areas need to be counted. Some businesses also count items that are transfers. These are products that were transferred to another location, or being delivered to a customer, but the item is still in their system. Most businesses count products that are on order, products that are in transfer outside the operations, and to customers, etc.

Many businesses have inventory that's kept in a mobile location, such as: Service trucks, sales person cars, etc. These items should be counted as well.

(d). When are you going to count?

It is very difficult to count inventory during a company's operating hours, this will be very hard to get an accurate count. Inventory counts should be performed during a company's off hours if possible (when a business is closed or before it opens for operation). Inventory count should have at least two or more managers performing inventory, this usually help make sure the inventory count is accurate, easier to double check any questionable counts, timely completion of the inventory count, this also help keep managers honest, etc. Some companies hire outside inventory companies to come in and perform their inventory. Most companies do their inventory with their own employees (management team).

CONTROLLING AND TRACKING INVENTORY

This section will review and explain account receivable invoice chart, primary report chart, par-level chart, performance summary report chart, inventory count sheet chart. All of the above that I mentioned has an important part in having a successful and profitable inventory.

Inventory is one of the main cores that keep most companies operating. Inventory can increase a company's business or decrease a company's business. When you keep accurate inventory records, you can tell whether you can take clients or customers request for orders, or meet particular projects with the inventory on hand. You can review the inventory records to identify products selling trends overtime (Par-Level Sheets) and make basic predictions about inventory that might run out faster than usual. Inventory records will help you plan and strategize your inventory at a successful level.

Inventory records are critical in developing and maintaining your company's relationship with investors. Investors want to see that a company has specific plans for their operations. A company that has good inventory records means that if customers shop, call, or write with inventory request or questions, you can quickly find the answer and give great customer satisfaction. When customers get a fast response to their question, it makes a good impression of the company.

When you know exactly what inventory you have on hand and where the inventory is stored, you can retrieve it quickly and fill the customer orders efficiently. The ability to have enough products, and fill orders quickly means the company is able to serve more customers and move more inventories through the company; this will result in higher profit. If customers have to wait for a response regarding an inventory request or wait for products, they may go to another company or cancel their orders.

Failure to maintain accurate inventory records can cause big losses for a company that work with dozens or even hundreds of customers every day. Sometimes companies end up ordering new inventory to meet their customers' demands; then later the company will find the original inventory and realize the new order wasn't necessary. This now cause the company to have more inventory than it needed, and the company also spent more money that was not necessary to spend (this is a profit drainer). Replacing products in this way is costly to a company, especially if the company can't sell the original inventory and ends up with extra product.

Inventory that is properly tracked provides a company the opportunity to measure its success. Successful inventory tracking can mean to some companies losing only one item per month. When the inventory staff meets this goal because they keep excellent inventory records, the staff should be given positive reinforcement and offered rewards. This help keep the employee's morale high, which often translates into better and stronger productivity and fewer conflicts.

Without good inventory records, a company can't tell whether their inventory staff deserves something extra or whether disciplinary action(written statement for poor performance) is appropriate.

A company that has accurate inventory records means that the inventory staff has more time available to do other important things to improve or keep inventory in control, such as: they can focus on new vendors, or come up with ideas and ways to reorganize the inventory for more efficiency and easy access. This will also improve the company's production. A company that implements inventory control can reduce the cost of running their business. This will improve customer service; and the best reason of all for controlling inventory is it makes the ordering process so much easier. Inventory control offers other benefits such as: Increased margins, keeps a fluid inventory, and also helps someone who is unfamiliar with the inventory records and task of ordering much easier. This will help anyone to be able to do the ordering more easily.

Ordering is also one of the keys to controlling inventory. Keeping accurate ordering records is very important.

Order Sheet = Is one of the keys to controlling inventory. A company uses an order sheet when they want to purchase products from other companies. An order sheet should include information needed to fill out the order sheet, such as;

- **(a).** The name of the company you are ordering your product from
- **(b).** The vendor's phone number
- **(c).** The time that the order was placed
- **(d).** The name of the vendor (contact person) who will be in charge of all your orders and who you can contact for any of your call in orders, and question about quality concern, and question for any price hikes in a product.
- **(e).** The product minimums of each order (what is the products minimum amount that you can order or what is the products maximum about that you can order)
- **(f).** The product price minimums of each order (what is the less dollar amount that you have to spend before a vendor will accept your order)
- **(g).** The date you are ordering the product should be at the top of the ordering column.

All products should be divided into the proper department, location, and section in which the product is kept. Make sure to leave room on each ordering sheet for any additions in each section. Be sure to record the products quantity on hand first before you do any ordering, and then order the product as needed according to the item par level.

Always indicate the items that are **out of stock** and items that are **discontinued**. This will take the guess work out of ordering. You will also know when to order, you will be able to reduce your inventory for any discontinued items, you will be able to reduce having any out of stock items, and help prevent over ordering.

Organizing your ordering process will also help your suppliers. It will be easier for your suppliers to maintain the necessary level of stock for you business, if your ordering process is consistent. Keep your order sheets in a file to create a historical record, and study all seasonal and yearly fluctuations in your company's sales. This information will inform you of which items to discontinue, determine product levels, shelf space for products, set sales goals for each department, and set guidelines for dealing with slow moving products. When you look at the previous order sheets, you can determine the potential volume of your sales.

When ordering product from a vendor it is important to determine the lead time necessary for ordering products. The **lead time** is the amount of time it takes to receive your product once your order has been placed to the vendor. The current stock of an item in your location should be running out just as the new shipment arrives. Most wholesalers (they provide products to a business) offer businesses computerized ordering systems to their retail accounts. These systems have many benefits such as;

(a).   It speeds the ordering process by eliminating long phone calls
(b).   Have product that have tag item numbers to identify each product
(c).   Have a description for each product
(d).   Use UPC code to make the item easier the scan or ring up at the register

MSI or other computerized systems that are purchased or leased from the wholesaler, and they will get their reimbursement through the business purchases.

Inventory turnover is directly related to a company's product margin and each department within the company contributes to the product margin. It costs money to carry an item in your business. If a product sits on your shelf for a long time, the more it will cost the company to sell that item. Slower moving items; such as body care items, have a higher margin than fast moving items. Fast moving items; such as dairy products have a lower margin. Inventory turnover and margins vary within each department, reflecting the volume of sales for each product category.

Example:

Pet shampoo may have a lower margin compared to pet conditioner, because of the difference in sales volume and inventory turnover.

Below is a similar formula that is used for determining the contributions to margin. If you were reviewing and examining the margin contribution of each department within your business, the chart may look similar to the chart below.

Note: This chart shows inventory in categories in each department

DEPARTMENT	MARGIN	X(TIMES)	% OF SALES	=	CONTRUBUTION
Produce	41%	X	21%	=	8.6%
Dairy	24%	X	13%	=	3.1%
Grocery	34%	X	42%	=	14.3%
Shoes	32%	X	40%	=	12.8%
Vitamins	35%	X	14%	=	4.9%
Body care	26%	X	18%	=	4.7%

Gross Margin 48.4%

*This formula is used for determining the contribution to margin:

Margin x Percent of Total Sales = Margin Contribution

*Most Inventory Managers want to order and buy extra of a product that is on sale by the supplier, and sell it at the regular price to make extra margin. The most common rule for inventory ordering is to make sure **NOT TO BUY MORE** than a month's worth of inventory and if they order a month of inventory they need to be sure it is only on high volume items (Fast moving items).

ACCOUNT RECEIVABLE

INVOICE FROM VENDOR (PRODUCE)

ITEMS	CASE	PRICE	TOTAL PRICE
5 X 6 Tomatoes	2	$12.50	$25.00
Roma Tomatoes	3	$11.00	$33.00
Sweet Potatoes	4	$9.50	$38.00
Carrots (50 Pound Bag)	1	$15.00	$15.00
Strawberries (Flat Box)	1	$13.00	$13.00
Lettuce	2	$17.00	$34.00

TOTAL INVOICE			**$158.00**

* **ITEMS column=** shows what product was ordered

* **CASE column=** is how many cases of the product that was ordered.

* **PRICE column=** shows the case price of each product

* **TOTAL PRICE column=** shows the total price of each product that was ordered

* TOTAL INVOICE= this is the total price of all the products that was ordered

*IMPORTANT TIPS

*Always double check your Invoice for wrong prices and wrong totals.

*Make sure all items **arrived** & **not damaged** (If product did not arrive or if product is damaged **subtract** the items from the invoice. **Make sure you have the vendor who delivered the products to sign & initial after adjustments are made to the invoice.**

*Make sure all items are in good condition to sell.

*Make sure that everything you ordered is on the invoice.

*Check for hike (increase) in prices

*Input invoice in the computer system quickly and accurate. This is to make sure all inventory is in the system for accurate inventory results.

*Make sure all the invoice prices and the amount of products received balance in your computer system for accurate inventory results and counts.

*IMPORTANT NOTE: When the vendor delivers products to your company; and you check all items and realize that one of these items are missing subtract that item from the invoice. **Example:** If the 2 cases of 5X6 Tomatoes didn't arrive; subtract the price of the 2 cases of 5x6 Tomatoes ($158.00 - $25.00 = $133.00) from the invoice. **Then adjusted invoice price to $133.00; and have the vendor sign or initial the adjustment on the invoice; this will verify that 2 cases of 5X6 Tomatoes didn't arrive at your company; therefore the company will not pay for the missing product.**

INVENTORY

UNDERSTANDING ITEMS ON AN ACCOUNT RECEIVABLE INVOICE

When receiving invoices from vendors make sure of the following:

(a). Always check to see if everything that was ordered is on the invoice. This is to make sure that no additional item was added to your invoice by the vendor that was not ordered. This can impact your ending inventory budget (Decrease Company's profit).

(b). Always check invoice for wrong prices, incorrect totals, and price hikes. This is to make sure that you review and calculate the invoice to make sure the company was not over charged for an item. At the time of your delivery check for products that are damaged, not received or not useable for sale; if one of these items are not useable for sale; subtract the cost (adjust the price) of the product that is not useable or the product that did not arrive from the invoice and have the vendor initial and sign were the price deduction was made. When entering this invoice in your company's computer system don't enter the product that was subtracted from the invoice; but make sure the adjusted price on the invoice balance in the system. This will save the company a lot of money and improve profits.

(c).   Always make sure all items arrive! Always check and count all products to insure that all products arrived. The most common mistake that businesses make is when they sign the received invoice and don't review and count all products that were delivered by the vendor; then they realize too late that one of the products on the invoice they signed was not delivered to the business.

At this point it's too late, the vendor don't have to give the business any money back (credit the company's account) on the product they didn't receive. The business will have to pay for a product that they didn't receive. This is a revenue and inventory lost for the business; this is a profit lost. This will also produce disappointing inventory results.

*Note: All items that are damage can't be sold and the company can't profit off damage product. If a vendor doesn't reimburse the business for the damage product, you will have to take the damage product off your next inventory count.

This means that the business will have to pay for a product that they can't sell.

When Invoices are entered in the computer system; the computer system must match the invoices (NO EXCEPTIONS).

Example: The invoice for produce is $158.00 you should enter each produce item in the computer and the total price that appears on the computer should add up to $158.00. If the computer total does not match the $158.00, then you will have to review each item that you entered into the computer and see which item was entered wrong or you may need to adjust one of the items price to the correct price on the invoice.

If you are in the food industry you need to be sure how your company counts each item during inventory. This is very helpful for entering account receivable items in the computer.

Example: Most companies count their items by the each, pint, pounds, quarts, bags, case, flats, etc. This is extremely important for inventory to balance and have profitable results.

Example A: If your company receives a 50lb bag of carrots, the company may count their carrots by the pound. You will have to put the carrots on a scale every time you count inventory; then record the carrots in your inventory by the pound.

Example B: If your company counts their 50lb bag of carrots by the each, you will have to count the carrots by the bag. You will count the bag this way = .1, .2, .3, .4, .5, .6, .7, .8, .9, 1. The 1 stands for a whole bag (the bag has not open).

.5 means a half of bag; anything less than .5 is under half; anything over a .5 is more than half.

Example C: If your company receives 1 case of sour cream; and there are 4 gallons to each case; and each case cost $10.00. If the company counts the sour cream by the gallon; you will have to enter 4 gallons in the computer system. The price you will enter in the computer system for each gallon is $2.50. ($10.00 (divided by) 4 = $2.50). Each gallon of sour cream is $2.50.

Example D: If your company receives 5 cases of sour cream; and there are 4 gallons to each case; each case cost $10.00.

*If the company counts the sour cream by the gallon; you will enter 20 gallons

(4 x 5 = 20) in the computer system; this is because 4 gallons of sour cream is in each case; and you received 5 cases of sour cream. The price you will enter in the computer system is $2.50. ($10.00 (divided by) 4 = $2.50

Note: Review how your company counts each of its products and then practice until you become familiar with how each product is counted.

Example E: If your company receives 4 cases of ketchup; and there are 6 gallons to each case; each case cost $9.75. If the company counts the ketchup by the gallons; you will enter 24 gallons (6 x 4 = 24) in the computer system; the price you will enter is $1.63 ($9.75 (divided by) 6 = $1.63.

Note: Every item that you enter in the computer system must be accurate in quantity and price in order for the computer system to balance with the company's inventory.

ACCOUNT RECEIVABLE

INVOICE FORM VENDOR (DAIRY & FOOD)

ITEMS	DESCRIPTION	CASE	PRICE	TOTAL PRICE
Sour Cream	Gallon (4 to Case)	5	$10.00	$50.00
Ranch Dressing	Gallon (4 to Case)	3	$9.00	$27.00
Mayonnaise	Gallon (4 to Case)	7	$11.00	$77.00
Honey	Gallon (6 to Case)	2	$8.75	$17.50
Ketchup	Gallon (6 to Case)	4	$9.75	$39.00
Butter	Pint (12 to Case)	2	$12.00	$24.00

TOTAL ITEMS = 6   **TOTAL CASES=23 TOTAL   PRICE=$234.50**

TAX: $ 23.45

SHIPMENT: $25.00

TOTAL PRICE DUE: $282.95

ITEMS COLUMN= shows what product was ordered

DESCRIPTION= describes the size, weight, etc. of the product; and it shows the number of products in each case.

CASE COLUMN= is how many cases of the product that was ordered

PRICE COLUMN= shows the case price of each product

TOTAL PRICE COLUMN= shows the total price of each product that was ordered

TOTAL ITEMS= the total number of items ordered

TOTAL CASES= the total number of cases that was ordered

TOTAL PRICE= the total price of all the products that was ordered

TAX= the tax the company must pay on the items ordered **(never enter the tax or shipment price when entering invoices in the computer system; only enter the total price of the items ordered).**

SHIPMENT= the price the company pay for having the order delivered by freight or shipment.

TOTAL PRICE DUE= the total price the company has to pay to the vendor or supplier.

Tips for Dairy and Food Invoice: Explain

*Some companies put their inventory in the system by the Each, Pints, Gallon, Case, Bags, or Pounds in the Food Industry.

*Make sure all items arrived

*Make sure all items are in good condition to sell, (If not reject item & subtract from invoice)

*Always check invoice for wrong prices and totals.

*Make sure all the items on the invoice is what you ordered.

*Check for hike in prices

*Put the invoice in the computer system as quickly as possible and accurately for accurate inventory results.

*Make sure invoice balance in the system; this is important for inventory count.

IMPORTANT NOTE: Sour Cream, Butter, and other related items are usually in the dairy section in the food industry.

Ranch Dressing, Mayonnaise, Honey and Ketchup are usually in the food section in the food industry.

Meat items are usually in the meat section in the food industry.

Many companies have different sections and departments; and each section and department must have accurate inventory and should be closely monitored at all times for the best inventory results that will increase profit.

WHAT TO LOOK FOR: EXAMPLE:

*Your store started the week with 5 cases of sour cream, which is 20 Gallons of sour cream. If you only have 3 Gallons of sour cream left at your Week End Inventory, and the computer said you only sold 10. (This mean 7 gallons of sour cream are missing).

What do this mean? DOUBLE CHECK ALL THE FOLLOWING:

*Was the item entered into the computer correctly? (Check your Invoice & also check what you entered into the system).

*Did the inventory staff check all 5 cases during the time of delivery to make sure all 5 cases actually came in the store?

*Did you count the sour cream wrong during your inventory count?

*Did the items not get rung up at the register?

*Do you have a theft problem?

TIPS TO TROUBLESHOOTING THE SOUR CREAM THAT ARE MISSING FROM INVENTORY:

 *1. Carefully recount the sour cream to make sure the sour cream was counted correctly. This includes all sour cream throughout the location (store) such as; in the coolers, in work stations, warehouse, and any other area in the store that sour cream is stored. An incorrect count of an item is one of the common mistakes during the inventory counting process. *If your count is correct and the ending count is 3 gallons of sour cream; you must enter 3 in the computerized inventory system or in the inventory bookkeeping records.

*DO NOT PAD OR FUDGE NUMBERS (Record False Count or Numbers)!! This will only cause more inventory problems in the future; and will most likely end your employment with the company.

 *(A). If (7) gallons of sour cream are missing from the business, the business just lost $17.50 in Food Cost (Revenue). ($2.50 X 7 = $17.50).

*Remember = Missing inventory will greatly impact a company's cost of sales, (decrease in money) and profit.

Companies that has frequent missing inventory that can't be controlled will eventually go into bankruptcy or close its business. This is why it is very important to troubleshoot and find a quick solution **(Game Plan)** to stop missing inventory within a business as soon as possible. **(No exceptions)**

*2. Check & review the sour cream's Account Receivable Invoice and make sure the correct number of sour cream was entered or recorded into the receiving inventory. This is also a common mistake that is found during troubleshooting inventory. Check the invoice to see who signature is on the invoice. This will tell you who checked in the sour cream and received the sour cream. Then check with that person to make sure all the sour cream on the invoice actually arrived, or did they send any sour cream back to the vendor for any reason such as; damaged, out of date, etc. This is another common mistake that some people forget to report or record on the invoice; they may even forget to record this information in the inventory report or the inventory computer system.

*Also check to see if the store transferred any sour cream to a sister store (another store that the company owns). Another store might have borrowed some sour cream from your store, but it was not recorded properly. This is another common mistake that may need troubleshooting. If this is the case, this can be easily adjusted in the inventory records.

*If none of the above solves the problem, you will have to troubleshoot the sour cream even deeper!!

*1. Check, review, and talk with staff members to see if any sour cream was broken, or thrown away due to damage or spoilage. This is why most companies should have a **Waste Sheet.** This is a sheet that everyone should record all items that can't be sold due to damages, spoilage, and breakage, over cooked (burned), out dated, waste that can't be sold, etc. A waste sheet keeps track of items that will be missing on the inventory count. This is a good tool to use in most companies. Some high volume stores use a big barrel to put waste items in each day and they count everything in the barrel during business hours and after the business close the store for the night, or during the slowest part of a shift. Most companies use a new waste sheet for every beginning inventory period and they keep this sheet until the end of an inventory period. All waste sheets should be kept in a file with inventory records. Waste Sheets is also a good tool for a company to know how much of its items are being wasted each week, month, and year. Controlling wasted items should be a priority every day. Too much wasted product will impact the company's revenue and profits.

*This sheet gives a business an eye opener and also gives the company the opportunity to prepare an Action Plan on how to solve and control the waste problem immediately.

SOME WAYS TO TROUBLE SHOOT AND MONITOR INVENTORY

*1. Missing inventory could also be a sign of a theft problem within the store.

(a). Inventory Managers need to be sure to monitor and review security tape for frequently missing products and to watch for theft.

(b). Inventory Managers must be aware daily of all products that are being received in the store, products being sold, or products that exit the store due to theft.

(c). Monitor and review the inside of all trash cans or bags before employees make a trash run. This is to make sure that product or the company's valuables are not going out the door along with the trash.

(d). Make sure all departments, coolers, freezers, stock rooms, office supply room, warehouse, back door, etc. are well organized, neat, and easy to monitor count. This makes the management team be able to quickly notice any products or items that are in areas that may cause for concern (Red Flag).

Example: If a good case of chicken breast is sitting by the back door along with the trash pile with other empty boxes; and the chicken box have chicken in it; this is a sign of a theft problem. This is why all boxes should be broken down before they are taken outside to the trash bin or recycle bin.

Example: If a new pair of shoes from the shoe department are in the office supply room stash in a corner; this is a sign of a theft problem. (Red Flag)

(e). Monitor (walkthrough) all registers to make sure that all products are being rung up at the register. Make sure all cashiers are ringing up all items at all times; no items can be given away for free at anytime.

(f). For anyone working in the food industry you should make sure all hot and cold food are at the correct temperature at all times; this will also control food cost and it is also excellent for your store when the health department visits. Make sure all measuring utensils are being used at all times when required. (No Exceptions). Using all required measuring utensils are very important. Most people who have worked in the food industry for a long time think that they don't have to use measuring utensils, because they think they can measure with their heads and hands just as good as a measuring utensil, or they can pour the correct amount of liquid exactly like a measuring cup or jigger (used for measuring alcohol beverages). Many employees will not use measuring utensil; but the truth is if measuring utensils are not being used it will definitely reduce the company's profit and revenue.

*When business allow employees to measure without the proper measuring utensils this will drive the food cost average very high. The company will spend more money on items that are required to be measured for recipes, because the items will run out quicker when they are not being measured. A company can make more profit and revenue if this system is in place.

Example: Someone has to use 1 cup of milk in a recipe; if they just pour the milk until they think they poured 1 cup of milk in the recipe; this can cause the recipe not to taste exactly the same as the recipe that was measured correctly. If everyone measured products based on what they think is 1 cup and not by using the proper measuring cup; the business will have an inventory control problem.

(g). When a company has a trend of missing items in the inventory; the company should start counting inventory more frequently within an accounting period.

Example: If you count inventory **once a week;** you need to count the items that has a missing trend **twice a week;** if the missing items are still not in control, you need to count the items **Three times a week** or maybe **every day** until the missing items are under inventory control.

(h). Need to check and review cashier's register tape or journal daily and weekly. The journal tape will show how much of each item was sold daily, weekly, and monthly. This is a good tool for tracking inventory items.

(i). Many businesses feel certain that shoplifting is not a problem in their business. Others are aware that the least suspected people can be robbing the business blind. This lesson is often learned through experience.

NOTE: Retailers are often surprised to find that they have more theft problems from employees than from shoplifters.

NOTE: A company should take basic precautions to prevent theft within the business. A business operation goal should be to keep the honest people honest. It is easier to prevent shoplifting than it is to catch a shoplifter.

There are many different ways a company can trouble shoot inventory. There are also many ways to track and control inventory. Tracking and controlling inventory will increase sales and profit for many companies.

ACCOUNT RECEIVABLE

INVOICE FROM VENDOR (RETAIL)

SELLING PRICE	ITEM	DESCRIPT. ITEM#	EACH	PRICE	TOTAL PRICE
$18.00 ea.	BK. Jumpsuit	048762987	20	$7.50	$150.00
$9.00 ea.	BL. Jumpsuit	0997897	30	$3.00	$90.00
$8.00 ea.	WH. Ruffle Shirt	0229299	15	$2.00	$30.00
$28.00 ea.	Gym BK. Sneaker	09921678	15	$7.00	$105.00
$15.00 ea.	BK. Bow Shoes	0123456	40	$5.00	$200.00
$5.00 ea.	PK. House Shoes	0244489	10	$1.00	$10.00
$10.00 ea.	BK/WH Curtains	01823482	25	$2.00	$50.00
$1.75 ea.	Bleach	Gallon(4 to Case)	8	$2.00	$16.00

TOTAL PRICE= $651.00

TAX: $23.80
SHIPMENT: $54.00
TOTAL PRICE: $728.80

Selling Price = This is the price that the company is selling the item for on the sales floor.

Item = This description of the item that is being sold

Description Item Number (#) = This is the UPC number that is printed on the tag; this tag is attached to the item, so the item will be easier to scan at the register.

Each = This is the number of each item that the company ordered.

Price = This is the price that the company paid the vendor or supplier for each item (wholesale price).

Total Price = This is the total price for each item that the company ordered from a vendor or supplier.

INVENTORY COUNT SHEET

SELL PRICE	WEEK 2 BEGINING INVEN.	RECEIV.	WEEK 2 INVEN. INVEN	TOTAL IN ENDING INVEN. SOLD	WEEK 2 ITEMS INCOME	WEEK 2 $ INVEN.	WEEK 2
BK. Jumpsuit							
$18.00 ea.	6	20	26	15	11		$198.00
BL. Jumpsuit							
$9.00 ea.	5	30	35	5	30		$270.00
WH. Ruffle Shirt							
$8.00 ea.	2	15	17	10	7		$56.00
Gym BK. Sneakers							
$28.00 ea.	3	15	18	7	11		$308.00
BK. Bow Shoes							
$15.00 ea.	7	40	47	14	33		$495.00
PK. House Shoes							
$5.00 ea.	1	10	11	6	5		$25.00
BK/WH Curtains							
$10.00 ea.	4	25	29	20	9		$90.00
Bleach							
$1.75	8	32	40	28	12		$21.00

TOTAL $ AMOUNT SOLD= $1,463.00

Sell Price = This is the price the company is selling the item for on the sales floor.

(Week 2) Beginning inventory = This is the beginning of a new accounting period. This shows how much each item has in the entire store at the beginning of an inventory period.

(Week 2) Receive Inventory = This is the number amount of each product that was delivered to the business by a vendor or supplier.

(Week 2) Total Inventory = This is the total of each items Ending Inventory + Received inventory. **Example: BK Jumpsuit (6 + 20 = 26) (26 is the total inventory)**

(Week 2) Ending Inventory = This is the amount of each item that is in the entire store (remaining items) after the end of the inventory count for the period end.

(Week 2) Items Sold = This is the total number of each items that was sold during week 2 of the inventory period.

(Week 2) = Inventory Income = This is the total dollar ($) amount of each item that was sold during the inventory period of week 2.

REVIEW THE CHART FOR THE FOLLOWING:

*Total Inventory Income the company made for Week 2 = $1,463.00

Each item on the chart Total Inventory Income is calculated by multiplying the **(week 2) Items Sold X the (Week 2) Selling Price = (Week 2) Inventory Income**

Example:

  (a)   **BK Jumpsuit** = Items Sold (11) X Selling Price ($18.00) = $198.00 Inventory Income. (11X$18.00 = $198.00)
  (b)   **BL Jumpsuit** = Items Sold (30) X Selling Price ($9.00) = $270.00 Inventory Income. (30X $9.00 = $270.00)

*Review the chart until you become familiar with it. Review your company's Inventory Count Sheet; so you can get familiar with all the items on the company's inventory count sheet.

*The company profit for Week 2 is = $728.80 – $1,463.00 = $734.20(Profit)

Explain: Remember the company's total Account Receivable Invoice from Vendor (Retail) was $728.80. This is the total amount of money the company paid for all the items on the invoice; Then the company sold and made $1,463.00 from the items on the invoice. This means the company made a profit of $ 734.20.

*What if the register tape show for Week 2, that the company **only sold 20** (BL Jumpsuit)? (This means that **10** of the BL Jumpsuits are **missing**)

*How do you track this? **EXPLAIN (Review the section) = Some Ways To Trouble Shoot and Monitor Inventory:**

*How do you keep this from happening again?

*This also means that the company lost $30.00 dollars for the cost of this item

The wholesale price for BL Jumpsuit is $3.00 X10= $30.00 (Review Invoice)

*This also means that the company lost $90.00 in Sales

The sales floor price (Retail Price) is $9.00 x 10 = $90.00 (Review Invoice)

SHORT EXAMPLE OF AN (PRIMARY REPORT) OR SOME CALL THIS A (SUMMARY REPORT) FOR A RETAIL STORE (IT MAY LOOK SIMULAR TO THIS CHART) (FOR THE MONTH OF SEPTEMBER 2014)

	Total Primary	Store A	Store B	Store C	Store D	Store E
Accessories	343,145	65,917	88,312	42,087	68,629	78,200
Apparel	382,750	96,400	60,942	80,846	86,462	58,100
Books	255,096	50,256	67,411	39,100	51,342	46,987
Electrical	360,371	80,700	82,348	32,728	88,275	76,320
Furniture	387,277	99,200	92,148	69,782	69,437	56,710
Shoes	370,191	71,692	81,402	56,100	87,808	73,189
Wares	368,173	87,546	72,992	64,000	73,629	70,006
Ornaments	39,316	10,492	15,120	556.00	6,006	7,142
Charity	1,814	350.00	108.00	782.00	264.00	310.00
Beer	110,331	27,640	28,640	18,214	20,100	15,738
Total Sales	**2,618,464**	**590,193**	**589,423**	**404,195**	**551,952**	**482,702**
		Store A	**Store B**	**Store C**	**Store D**	**Store E**
Budget Sales Real	1,762,100	600,000	540,220	395,000	540,100	526,100
Difference Total	+856,365	-9,907	+49,203	+9,195	+11,852	-43,398
Sales Last Year	1,120,100	510,100	520,100	380,000	500,000	520,000
Labor Hours	161,175	34,562	37,879	23,044	31,910	33,780
Labor Hours Last Year	185,254	48,229	42,602	26,415	37,189	30,819

*A Primary Report gives the company and Managers an overall look at how well the Store, Region, and District are performing.

***Note:** This report is commonly used weekly, monthly, and yearly

***Please review the chart** and review how good or how bad each store is performing in each category.

***Let's review the Primary Chart and do a short quiz!!**

Total Primary = This column shows all the stores that the company owns and it shows the total dollar ($) amount of sales for all stores A, B, C, D, and E added (+) together in each category for the month of September.

Example: In the Accessories row= All stores A-E total sales in Accessories added together is **$343,145;** this is the Total Primary sales in Accessories.

Example: In the Furniture row = All stores A-E total sales in Furniture added together is $387,277; this is the Total Primary sales in Furniture.

All the stores added together in this column (Total Primary) = **$2,618,465.** This is the total dollar amount of all stores added together.

A-E Stores = Each store has a column that shows how well each store did in sales in each category for the month of September.

Total Sales = This is the actual total dollar ($) amount of each store sales in each category for the month of September.

Example: Store A did **$590,193** in total sales for the month of September.

Example: Store B did $589,423 in total sales for the month of September.

Budget Sales = This is the projected sales goal (dollar amount) that the executive staff set and expect for each store to reach in the month of September. Each Store is expected to reach the Budget Sales goal that the company set.

Example: Store A Budget Sales is $1,762,100

Example: Store C Budget Sales is $395,000

Real Difference row = This is the difference in the dollar amount between **Total Sales and Budget Sales.** Subtract the Total Sales – from the Budget Sales = Real Difference.

Example: Store A total sales was ($590,193) – what the company's set **budget sales** was for Store A ($600,000 = -9,907 the **real difference.**

The Real Difference for Store A is -9,907, because the company wanted Store A to make $600,000 for the month of September; but Store A only made $590,193. This means that

Store A did not meet the company's sales goal expectation for September. Store A missed their sales goal by $-9,907.

Total Sales Last Year = This dollar ($) amount shows what each store did in sales last year in September. This tells the company if each store made more money or less money this year than last year.

*****Note:** You always want to make more money in the current year than last year. If your sales go up each year; this shows that the business is increasing in sales each year and increasing profit.

Labor Hours = This is the amount of labor hours that each store employees worked in the month of September this year.

Example: Store A employees worked **34,562 hours** in the month of September.

Example: Store E employees worked **33,780 hours** in the month of September.

Example: The total Labor Hours for all Stores combined is **161,175.**

Labor Hours Last Year = This is the amount of Labor Hours that each store spent last year in the month of September.

Example: Store A employees worked 48,229 hours last year in the month of September. This means that Store A spent less labor hours this year in September; than it did last year in September. Store A did better in labor hours this year than last year.

This is a review quiz of the Primary Report!! Answers on the next page!!

1. Which store made more money in Accessories?
2. Which store made more in Electrical?
3. Which store made less in shoes?
4. Which store made less in beer?
5. What is the Budget Sales for Store B?
6. What is the Total Sales for Store E?
7. What are the Labor Hour hours for Store C?
8. Which store missed their Budget Sales the most?
9. Which store went over their Budget Sales?
10. Did the company as a whole go over their Budget Sales? If so, how much did they go over their Budget Sales?
11. How much Total Sales Last Year did the company make as a whole?
12. How much Total Sales in the current Year did the company make as a whole?

ANSWERS TO THE REVIEW QUIZ

1. **Store B made more in Accessories than the others; Store B made 88,312.**
2. **Store D made more in Electrical than the others; Store D made 88,275.**
3. **Store C made less in shoes than the others; Store C made 56,100.**

4. **Store E made less in beer than the others; Store E made 15,738.**
5. **540,220** are the company's projected Budget Sales for Store B.
6. **482,702** are the Total Sales for Store E.
7. **23,044** are the Labor Hours for Store C.
8. **26,415** are the Last Year Labor Hours for Store C.
9. **Store E missed their Budget Sales the most.**
10. **Yes** the company as a whole did go over the company's Budget Sales; The company went over their Budget Sales by **+856,365.**
11. **1,120,100** were the Total Last Year Sales that the company made as a whole.
12. **2,618,465** are the current Total Sales that the company made as a whole.

HOW TO ORDER INVENTORY ACCORDING TO SALES

*1. Most companies have a **Par Level** (How much of each item is needed at each store). This is based on the weekly or monthly sales trend of each item.

*2. **EXAMPLE:** If the company requires a unit (store) to have 50 gallons of milk each week, this is called a Par Level. If you only have 34 gallons of milk left at the end of the week after your end inventory count; then you only need to re-order 16 gallons of milk from your assigned vendor. **EXAMPLE:**

STORE ITEMS	BEGINNING ON HAND	ENDING COUNT	TOTAL SOLD	ORDER NEEDED	PAR LEVEL
Milk (6 in Case)	50	34	16	16	50
American Cheese (Each)	30	3	27	32	35
Sour Cream (6 in Case)	15	0	15	30	30
Orange Juice (6 in Case)	42	2	40	38	40
Bag Potatoes (Each)	10	6	4	2	8
Mash Potatoes (6 in Case)	7	3	4	3	6
Eggs (Each)	15	2	13	11	13
Minne Lite (24 in Case)	62	4	58	56	60
N.K Kirbys (24 in Case)	48	7	41	45	52

White Vodka (6 in Case)	.5	1.3	.2	0	1
Brown Vodka (6 in Case)	.4	0	.4	4	4

* What if some item on the chart can only be ordered by the case?

*Each case has 6 items to a case

Example: Milk = You only need to order 16 gallons of milk; you will only need to order 3 cases of milk for the business; this will be **18 gallons of milk.** (6X3= 18)

***DO NOT** order 2 cases of milk for the business, because this will only be 12 gallons of milk; which means the business will run out of milk before the end of the week, or before the next milk delivery arrive. This could result in unhappy customers, and decrease in sales and profits. (Red Flag)

***Note: You can order a little over par-level; but never order less than the par-level!**

Example: White Vodka = The beginning count was .5; the store did not have any deliveries received (means 0 White Vodka came in the store) for this period; the ending inventory count is 1.3;

Explanation: The beginning count was .5 and the ending count 1.3; there was no white vodka delivered to the store; this means that the 1 bottle of white vodka that was counted this inventory period, was not counted last inventory period. This means that the Inventory Managers over looked the 1 bottle of white vodka last inventory period. This also means that the business took a lost in revenue for the 1 bottle that was not counted last week; but the business took a gain in revenue this week for finding the 1 bottle of white vodka; this may sound o.k., because the business did find and count the bottle this inventory period; but the truth is This is Not Good for business. This could also mean that someone took the 1 bottle of White Vodka out of the store last inventory period; then replaced the 1 bottle of White Vodka this inventory period. **This is called Theft!!**

This is why inventory should be counted very carefully and correctly at all time, to keep from making this mistake; and keep theft from happening.

Example: White Vodka ending count is 1.3; the business only sold .2 of White Vodka; the Par Level for White Vodka is 1; this means that White Vodka don't have to be ordered this inventory period, because the store still has 1.3 remaining in the store.

***Practice and review this chart until you get familiar with it.**

PAR- LEVEL = To create a par level for each item or product; you must carefully look at the weekly and monthly sales trend or the usage for each item or product. You should go back and review the item sales for at least four or five months. After reviewing the sales trend for an item; then set the par level for the item.

*If you review all inventory report for the past five months; this will show you items sold history report.

Example: After reviewing the past five months of the inventory reports; you might see that milk has a weekly trend of selling 45 – 48 gallons of milk each week. The Par Level should be set at 60 gallons of milk a week. This gives you a little more extra milk in the store. This way you are prepared for any extra business from customers. Par Level is a good tool for most companies; par level helps the company control their inventory level, prevent over ordering and over stock, helps reduce spoilages in product and also help reduce theft.

LET'S TALK ORDERING AND PAR- LEVELS (WEEK 1)
THIS CHART MAY BE SIMULAR TO A ORDER CHART IN A BUSINESS
Each Product Name shows underneath it; exactly what's in each case

Product Name	On Hand	Week 1 End Count	Week 1 Total Sold	Week 1 Total Needed	Par Level	Total Items Ordered	Item Price	Total Price Order
Milk (Gal.) (4 in Case)	50	34	16	26	60	7 Cases	$10.00	$70.00
Cheese (Each)	30	3	27	32	35	32 Ea.	$2.00	$64.00
Sour Cream (12 in Case)	15	0	15	40	40	4 Cases	$12.00	$48.00
Apple Juice (4 in Case)	42	2	40	38	40	10 Cases	$11.00	$110.00
Potatoes (50lb. Bag)	10	6	4	2	8	2 Bags	$7.00	$14.00
Eggs (Each)	15	2	13	11	13	11 Ea.	$1.50	$16.50
Brown Beer (24 in Case)	62	4	58	56	60	3 Cases	$13.00	$39.00
Clear Beer (24 in Case)	48	7	41	45	52	2 Cases	$8.00	$16.00
White Wine (12 in Case)	21	5	16	13	18	2 Cases	$2.00	$4.00
Dark Wine (12 in Case)	36	3	33	32	35	3 Cases	$2.50	$7.50
Ruffle Shirt (10 in Case)	30	20	10	0	20	0	$20.50	0

	On Hand	Ending Count	Total Items Sold					
Pink Jeans (10 in Case)	50	20	30	15	35	2 Cases	$25.00	$50.00
Blue Jeans (10 in Case)	70	40	30	0	30	0	$25.00	0
Gold Watch (Each)	15	2	13	11	13	11 Ea.	$4.00	$44.00
Purple Watch (Ea.)	60	40	20	0	25	0	$4.00	0
Green Shoes (6 Pair Case)	25	20	5	0	15	0	$6.00	0
Yellow Shoes (6 Pair Case)	50	20	30	10	30	2 Cases	$6.00	$12.00
TOTAL	629	228	401	331		91 Items		$495.00

Let's Review the Inventory Chart for Week 1

ON HAND = This is the beginning inventory count of items that are in the business (remaining) at the beginning of a starting period.

ENDING COUNT = This is the ending inventory count of items at the end of an inventory period. This is the final number of items that was counted at the end of the inventory process. These are the items remaining in the store after inventory is complete.

TOTAL ITEMS SOLD = This is the amount of items sold within the business within a time period.

*You can find out the total items sold for Week 1 by: **Subtracting the On Hand – from the Ending Count = Total Items Sold**

Example: Milk = On Hand is 50 – 34 which is the ending count = 16 Total Items Sold in Week 1.

PAR- LEVEL = This is the company's set amount of each item that the company needs between a certain time period.

*If a company uses a Par- Level; at the end of the complete inventory count; they will **take the Par-Level and subtract it from the ending count.**

Example: Milk = Par-Level is 60 – 34 Ending Count = 26 Total items needed to be ordered.

TOTAL ITEMS NEEDED = This is the number of each item that the business need to order from the supplier or vendor.

Example: Milk = The total amount of milk that the business need to order is **26.**

TOTAL ITEMS ORDERED = This is the order that the business will call in to the supplier or send electronically to the supplier or vendor.

Example: Milk = The company counts milk by each gallon. The total amount of milk needed is 26; but the suppliers or vendors only deliver some items by the case; Milk has 4 gallons to each case; this means that the business have to order 7 cases of milk from the supplier. (4x 7= 28). The company will have to order 28 gallons of milk (7 cases) because if they order 6 cases (4X6= 24) that will only be 24 gallons of milk; that will not be enough because the par- level requires the business order 26 gallons of milk.

Note: A business can order an item a little over the par-level; but **NOT** order less of an item.

ITEM PRICE = The price the supplier or vendor charge for each of their items.

TOTAL PRICE = The total price of each item that was ordered by the business. This is also the total price that the business will have to pay the supplier or vendor for the items.

Review the Week 1 chart for the next example:

Example: Pink Jeans

Step 1: Pink Jeans has 10 pair Jeans in each case; subtract On Hand 50 – 20 Ending Count = 30 Total Item Sold. **(50-20=30).**

Step 2: Subtract the Ending Count – Par-Level = Total Item Needed to be ordered;

(35 – 20 = 15).

Step 3: You need to order 15 pair of Pink Jeans; but the Pink Jeans has 10 pair jean in each case; you will order 2 Cases (20 Pair Pink Jeans); (10 X 2 = 20); because if you order 1 case, this is only 10 pair Pink Jeans; but your Par-Level require that you order 15 pair Pink Jeans; so you will have to order 20 (2 cases); this is a little over what you need, but it is better to have a little more of an item, than a little less of an item.

Please review the (Week 1) Chart until you are familiar with the ordering process and par-levels.

LET'S TALK ONE (1) MORE ORDERING AND PAR-LEVELS FOR (WEEK 2)

- **PLEASE REVIEW THE CHART ON WEEK 1; WEEK 2 IS A CONTINUATION FROM WEEK 1:**
- **WEEK 2 BEGINNING HAND COUNT IS WEEK 1 ENDING COUNT**

*WE WILL ALSO REVIEW ORDERS THAT WAS DELIVERED TO THE BUSINESS:

PRODUCT NAME	ON HAND HAND	ORDERS RECEIVED SOLD	TOTAL ON NEEDED	ENDING COUNT ORDERED	TOTAL ITEMS ORDERED	TOTAL ITEM VALUE	PAR LEVEL	TOTAL ITEMS	ITEM PRICE	TOTAL PRICE	TOTAL DOLLAR
MILK	34	28	62	5	57	55	60	14 CASES	$10.00	$140.00	$155.00
CHEESE	3	32	35	3	32	32	35	32	$2.00	$64.00	$70.00
SOUR CREAM	0	48	48	3	45	37	40	4 CASES	$12.00	$48.00	$48.00
APPLE JUICE	2	40	42	4	38	36	40	9 CASES	$11.00	$99.00	$115.00
POTATOES	6	2	8	3	5	5	8	5 BAGS	$7.00	$35.00	$56.00
EGGS	2	11	13	1	12	12	13	12	$1.50	$18.00	$19.50
BROWN BEER	4	72	76	8	68	52	60	3 CASES	$13.00	$39.00	$41.04
CLEAR BEER	7	48	55	7	48	45	52	2 CASES	$8.00	$16.00	$18.15
WHITE WINE	5	24	29	3	26	15	18	2 CASES	$2.00	$4.00	$4.93
DARK WINE	3	36	39	6	33	29	35	3 CASES	$2.50	$7.50	$8.19
RUFFLE SHIRT	20	0	20	10	10	10	20	1 CASE	$20.50	$20.50	$41.00
PINK JEANS	20	20	40	12	28	23	35	3 CASES	$25.00	$75.00	$100.00
BLUE JEANS	40	0	40	5	35	25	30	3 CASES	$25.00	$75.00	$100.00
GOLD WATCH	2	11	13	13	0	0	13	0	$4.00	0	$52.00
PURPLE WATCH	40	0	40	20	20	5	25	5	$4.00	$20.00	$160.00
GREEN SHOES	20	0	20	16	4	0	15	0	$6.00	0	$20.00
YELLOW SHOES	20	10	30	10	20	20	30	4 CASES	$6.00	$24.00	$30.00
BROWN SHOES	20	24	44	4	40	36	40	6 CASES	$6.00	$36.00	$44.00
TOTAL	248	406	654	133	521	437		108 CASES		$721.00	$1,083.31

PLEASE REVIEW THE CHART FOR WEEK 2 WHILE YOU ARE READING THE SECTION BELOW

WEEK 2

ON HAND = This is the beginning inventory count for Week 2. This count came from Week 1 Ending Count.

Example: The Milk Ending Count for Week 1 was 34; Milk beginning inventory count for Week 2 is 34.

Note: You continue this cycle weekly for each month, or monthly, or yearly; whichever your business assign for the period end.

ORDER RECEIVED = The items that you ordered from the supplier or vendor. These are the items that were delivered to your store during week 2; so you will add the On Hand + Order Received = Total on Hand for Week 2 (62)

34 + 28 = 62 (This will give you the total amount of items that are in your store for Week 2)

Example: Milk = 7 cases (28 gallons) of milk was delivered to your store; the 7 cases of milk will go in the order received column (28 gallons).

* Remember: Milk has to be ordered from the supplier by the case; but you will put milk in your order received column by the gallon.

TOTAL ON HAND = The total of all items in your store after all orders has been delivered and received.

Example: Milk= On Hand + Orders Received = Total On Hand

$$34 \quad + \quad 28 \quad = \quad 62$$

*The store now has 62 gallons of milk in the store for week 2.

ENDING COUNT = The ending inventory count for a period end. This means the ending count of each item that are in the store (items remaining in store) at the end of the inventory count or period.

Example: There are only 5 gallons of milk left in the store after inventory was counted for the period end of week 2.

TOTAL ITEMS SOLD= This is the total amount of items sold within the Week 2 period. Subtract the Total On Hand – Ending Count = Total Sold Items.

Example: Milk = Total On Hand – Ending Count = Total Sold Items.

$$61 \quad \quad 5 \quad \quad 57$$

*The store sold 57 gallons of milk in week 2.

TOTAL ITEMS NEEDED = This is the amount of each item that the store needs to order from its supplier or vendor.

Example: Milk = The total amount of milk that needs to be ordered for the store is 55; Subtract the Par-Level - Ending Count = Total Items Ordered

$$60 \quad - \quad 5 \quad = \quad 55$$

PAR-LEVEL = This is the company's set amount of each item that is needed in the store to last until the end of each time period.

TOTAL ITEMS ORDERED = This is the order that you will call in or send to the supplier or vendor.

Example: Milk = The company counts milk by each gallon; the total amount of milk ordered is 14 cases (56 gallons).

*Remember milk has 4 gallons of milk in each case (4 X 14 = 56).

You only need 55 gallons of milk; but you will have to order over the par-level a little in order to have enough milk for the store sales. If you ordered 13 cases

(4X 13= 52) this will not be enough; because you have to order 55 gallons of milk for the required par-level.

ITEM PRICE = This is the wholesale price that the supplier or vendor charge the business for each item.

TOTAL PRICE ORDERED = This is the total price of each item that was ordered. This is the Total Price Ordered that the business will have to pay the supplier or vendor.

TOTAL DOLLAR VALUE = This is the Total Dollar Value of each item that was in the store during week 2 (Total On Hand).

Example: Milk = One case of milk cost the business $10.00; each case of milk has 4 gallons of milk; each gallon of milk cost $2.50:

Divide 4 gallons of milk into $10.00 = $2.50. This means the business pays $2.50 for each gallon of milk.

Total on Hand X The Cost of Each Gallon of Milk = Total Dollar Value

$$62 \quad X \quad \$2.50 \quad = \quad \$155.00$$

*Total Dollar Value of milk is $155.00

WEEK 2

LET'S REVIEW ANOTHER ITEM ON THE CHART FOR WEEK 2 (GREEN SHOES)

GREEN SHOES = There are 6 pair of Green Shoes in each case.

ON HAND = The Green Shoes ending count for Week 1 was 20; Green Shoes beginning inventory count for Week 2 is 20.

ORDER RECEIVED = There was 0 (Zero) Green Shoes ordered for week 2; therefore there was NO Green Shoes delivered to the store for week 2;

TOTAL ON HAND = Green Shoes Total On Hand is 20; because

On Hand + Order Received = Total On Hand (20 + 0 = 20)

20 + 0 = 20

ENDING COUNT = There are 16 pair of Green Shoes left (remaining) in the store after inventory was counted for week 2.

TOTAL ITEMS SOLD = Green Shoes Total Item Sold is 4;

The On Hand - Ending Count = Total Item Sold (20 – 16 = 4)

20   16   4

TOTAL ITEMS NEEDED = The total amount of Green Shoes needed for the store is 0 (Zero); Subtract the Par-Level from the Ending Count = Total Items Needed

Par-Level – Ending Count = Total Items Needed

15   16   =   +   1

*+1 means the store has 1 to many in the store according to the Par-Level; so you **DO NOT** have to order any Green Shoes.

The par-level requires 15 pair Green Shoes in the store to last until the end of each time period; but the store has 16 pair Green Shoes; this is 1 pair Green Shoes to many.

PAR-LEVEL = This is the company's set amount of each item that is needed in the store to last until the end of each time period.

TOTAL ITEMS ORDERED = Total Items Ordered for Green shoes is 0; because the store has 1 to many according to the company's par-level.

ITEM PRICE = The wholesale price for a case of Green Shoes is $6.00

TOTAL PRICE ORDERED = Total price for Green Shoes is 0, because there was not any Green Shoes ordered.

TOTAL DOLLAR VALUE = One case of Green Shoes cost the company $6.00; each case of Green Shoes has 6 pairs; this means that each pair of Green Shoes cost $1.00; this means the company pays $1.00 for each pair Green Shoes.

Divide 6 pair shoes into $6.00 = $1.00; add (+) the Total On Hand 20 + the cost of Green Shoes $1.00 = $20.00; ($20.00 is the Total Dollar Value of the Green Shoes

WEEK 2

LET'S REVIEW ANOTHER ITEM ON THE CHART FOR MORE PRACTICE

(BROWN BEER)

BROWN BEER = This item has 24 bottle of brown beer in each case.

ON HAND = Brown Beer ending inventory count for Week 1 was 4; Brown Beer beginning count for Week 2 is 4.

ORDER RECEIVED = 72 bottles (3 cases) of brown beer was ordered and delivered at the store during week 2; the 3 cases of brown beer will go in the Order Received column; which is **72** bottles of brown beer.

*Remember = Brown Beer has to be ordered by the case; there are 24 bottles of beer in each case (24 X 3 = 72).

If the business ordered 2 cases of Brown Beer that would not be enough brown beer to reach the set par-level for brown beer (24 X 2 = 48). 48 are not enough; so this is why 72 bottle of brown beer was ordered; this is a little over the par-level; but its o.k. to go a little over par-level than to go less than the par-level.

TOTAL ON HAND = Brown Beer= On Hand + Order Received = Total On Hand

4   72   76

ENDING COUNT = The ending count for Brown Beer is 8 after inventory was counted for week 2.

TOTAL ITEMS SOLD = The total amount of Brown Beer that was sold is **68**.

On Hand - Ending Count = Total Items Sold

76   -   8   =   68

(4 + 72 = 76) ***76** is the total amount of Brown Beer bottles in the store.

TOTAL ITEMS NEEDED =The total amount of Brown Beer needed in the store is **52**. Par-Level - Ending Count = Total Items Needed

60   -   8 52

PAR-LEVEL = This is the companies set amount of each item that is needed in the store to last until the end of each time period. Brown Beer par-level is 60.

TOTAL ITEMS ORDERED = The company count Brown Beer by the each (each bottle). There was 72 bottle of Brown Beer ordered for the store.

The company only needs 52 bottles of Brown Beer to reach the par-level; but they had to order over the par-level a little in order to meet the par-level.

ITEM PRICE = This is the wholesale price for each item that the supplier or vendor charges the company. The item price for brown beer is $13.00.

TOTAL PRICE = The total price of each item that was ordered, this is the Total Price that the company has to pay the supplier or vendor.

TOTAL DOLLAR VALUE = This is the Total Dollar Value of all the items that are in the store during the week 2.

One case of brown beer cost the company $13.00; each case of brown beer has 24 bottles in it; this means that each brown beer bottle cost the company .54 cents; **Divide 24 into $13.00 = .54 Cents**

*The Total On Hand for brown beer is 76; (76 X .54 Cents = $41.04)

***$41.04 is the Total Dollar Value of Brown Beer.**

TOTAL DOLLAR VALUE FOR SOUR CREAM = One case of Sour Cream cost the company $12.00; each case of sour cream has 12 pints in it; this means that each pint of sour cream cost the company $1.00; **Divide 12 into $12.00 = $1.00**

The Total On Hand for sour cream is 48; (48 X $1.00 = $48.00)

$48.00 is the Total Dollar Value of Sour Cream.

TOTAL DOLLAR VALUE FOR CHEESE = Cheese is by the each; each pack of cheese cost the company $2.00; the Total Item On Hand for cheese is 35;

(35 X $2.00 = 70.00)

$70.00 is the Total Dollar Value of Cheese.

*Please review the week 1 and week 2 charts until you are familiar with the ordering, par-levels, prices and calculation for the inventory procedures and process.

*Both charts are similar to how most company's inventory chart will look. Most companies will use these charts once a week, once a month, or once a year.

LET'S TALK INVENTORY PROFIT

Most companies require the Inventory Manager and Inventory Staff to know how much each individual item cost. This is must know information to help track the cost of each item that is sold, returned, damaged or missing. The company can also keep track of how much money they are making from each item by reviewing their inventory records. The company needs to know how much each item cost the company so they can decide what price they will sell the item for on the sales floor.

Let's talk about how much items cost the company and how much the company's retail price will be for items, and what the company's profit will be for each item.

Note: Most companies will double or triple their retail price on an item that is sold to its customers. This is to make more profit from an item. Most companies do this to double and triple their profits quickly; but sometimes the price can be too high for the customers and they will buy the items from another business that is cheaper. This could hurt the company revenue also, if the price is too high.

Example: Milk = The company paid $2.50 for one gallon of milk; then the company priced the milk at $5.00 for the retail price; the company will make a profit of $2.50.

Explain: Retail Price - The Company's Cost = Company's Profit

$$\$5.00 \quad - \quad \$2.50 \quad = \quad \$2.50$$

($5.00 - $2.50 = $2.50)

The company is charging $5.00 for the milk; the company made their $2.50 back that they spent on the milk; then they made $2.50 extra; this is called **PROFIT**.

Example: Brown Beer = The company paid .54 Cents for each bottle of brown beer; then the company priced each bottle of brown beer at $2.00 for the retail price; the company will make a profit of $1.46.

Explain: Retail Price - The Company's Cost = Company's Profit

$$\$2.00 \quad - \quad .54\ Cents \quad = \quad \$1.46$$

($2.00 - .54 Cents = $1.46)

Review the week 2 chart for numbers 1 – 10

The bottom line on the Inventory Chart for Week 2 is the Total of each column.

1. The total amount of items On Hand in the entire store in week 2 is **654.**
2. **Total Orders Received** = The total number of all items that was delivered to the store in week 2. **(406)**
3. **Ending Count** =The total number of all items that are remaining in the store at the period end. **(133)**
4. **Total Items Sold** = The total number of all items that were sold in week 2. **(521)**
5. **Total Items Needed** = The total number of all items that the company needs to order. **(437)**
6. **Par-Level** = DO NOT have to be added, because it's just an ordering guide line for each item.
7. **Total Items Ordered** = The total number of all items that was ordered from the supplier or vendor. **(108)**
8. **Total Price** = DO NOT have to be added, because this is just a price list of each item.
9. **Total Price Ordered** = The total dollar amount that the company paid the vendor or supplier for all the items that was ordered in week 2. **($721.00)**
10. **Total Dollar Value of Items On Hand** = The total value dollar amount of all the items in the store during week 2. **($1,083.31)**

(WEEK 3) INVENTORY & PERFORMANCE SUMMARY REPORT (RESTAURANT)

(Store Name)	Crestway	Folly	Frattville	English Fort
Sales for Week	47,907	40,868	51,564	38,136
Last Year Sales	58,955	43,128	61,292	38,998
Up/Down $$	-11,048	-2,260	-9,728	-862
Up/Down %	-18.74%	-5.24%	-15.87%	2.21%
Customer Count This Year	6,240	5,263	6,112	4,689
Customer Count Last Year	7,821	5,789	7,756	4,949
Customer Count/+/-	-1,581	-526	-1,644	-260
Cost of Goods Sold	17,990	15,465	18,785	13,080
Food Cost	37.55%	37.84%	36.43%	34.30%
Prior Week Food Cost	37.20%	37.60%	35.70%	35.50%
Food Cost Target	38.50%	36.60%	36.60%	36.60%
Ending Inventory	18,531	17,791	16,066	17,108
Beverage %	71.00%	74.00%	77.40%	79.40%
Payroll Dollars	8,212	6,648	7,881	5,885
Cashier Hours	90	82	115	85
Server Hours	411	349	430	275
Other Hours	676	622	732	584
Total Hours	1,177	1,053	1,277	944
Overtime Hours	0	0	9	0
Cashier Hours	-18	-11	0	-1
Server Hours	-26	-27	-19	-64
Other Hours	-33	-9	11	-22

*Inventory and Performance Summary Report shows how well the company or each store is performing. It also shows if the company is meeting budget goals.

Store Name = Name of each store in the companies district.

Sales for Week = The total sales revenue each store earned in week 3.

Last Year Sales = The total sales revenue each store earned last year in the same week as this year.

Up / Down $$ = This is the difference in dollar amount between this year sales and last year sales.

Customer Count This Year = The number of customers that entered the store and purchased a meal this week in this current year.

Customer Count Last Year = The number of customers that entered the store last year in the same week as this week.

Customer Count/+/- = This is the number difference between the number of customers that entered into the store and purchased a meal this week and last year in the same week.

Cost of Goods Sold = The total cost of each item or product that was sold this week.

Food Cost = This is the ending inventory count; this count tells how well or how bad a business did in their food cost % to gauge how well the business is performing in food cost.

Prior Week Food Cost = This shows the store prior week food cost. The store can gauge how well they did in food cost % this week versus the prior week food cost%.

Food Cost Target = This is the food cost % goal that the executive staff set for each store to achieve.

*TIP TO REMEMBER = A store always want their food cost % target to be a little under the food cost % target that the company set for them. If a store go over their food cost %, that means the store need to monitor their inventory more closely. If a store is constantly not meeting or exceeding their company's food cost % goal; this will be a big problem; the company will have a huge lost in revenue and may have to close its doors for good; or file bankruptcy.

Ending Inventory = This is the dollar value amount of all the inventory that is remaining in the store after the ending inventory count.

Beverage % = This is the percent of all beverages that was sold in the store for the week.

Payroll Dollars = The total payroll dollars that a store spent on employees payroll for the week.

Cashier Hours = The total hours that all cashiers was scheduled and worked for the week.

Server Hours = The total hours that all servers was scheduled and worked for the week.

Other Hours = The total hours that other workers was scheduled and worked such as: cooks, maintenance, shift leaders, stockers, meat cutters, etc.

Total Hours = The total hours for the entire staff in a store that worked for the week.

Overtime Hours = The total overtime hours that was worked by any employee for the week.

Server Hours +/- = The number that shows if the server hours was under (-) or over (+) companies set payroll budget.

Other Hours = The number that shows if the other hours was under (-) or over (+) companies set payroll budget.

LET'S REVIEW THE STORES IN EACH DISTRICT ON THE INVENTORY & PERFORMANCE REPORT (RESTAURANT) WEEK 3

*1. The store that made the most sales for the week is Frattville; their sales for the week were **$51,564**.

*2. Frattville last year sales were $61,292; Frattville made more in sales last year in the same week than it did this year in the same week; which means Frattville made $9,728 less in sales this week than last year during the same week; Frattville is down in sales by 15.87%.

*3. The store that made less in sales for the week is English Fort; their sales for the week were $38,136.

*4. English Fort last year sales was $38,998; English Fort made more in sales last year in the same week than it did this year in the same week; which means English Fort made $862 less in sales this sales week than last year sales during this same week; English Fort sales is down by 2.21%.

*When a store or stores continue to decline in sales, this is NOT GOOD!

Declining sales should always be investigated quickly. A company should monitor very closely and get an action plan together on how they will increase the company's sales. The company should check for some of the following:

*(a) Have their store been having a lot of customers complaints of dissatisfaction with service, product, etc?

* (b) Are all the employees customer friendly and give good customer service?

*(c) Did the quality of the company's product decline?

*(d) Did the quality of the company's supplier or vendor decline?

*(e) Are all employees being very productive while at work or has production decline?

*(f) Are any machinery in the store broken or not working properly that may affect production?

*(g) Is the store neat, clean, and organized at all times?

*(h) Are the management team performing at high quality levels (100%) each day?

*(i) Did the store perform at the highest level?

*5. Folley's customer count this year was 5,263; their customer count last year was 5,789; this means that Folley customers count declined by -526 this year.

*NOTE: When a store is losing that many customers each period end, it is time for troubleshooting quickly, or the business will eventually have to close its doors or file for bankruptcy.

> ***6.** The cost of goods sold is the price that the company paid for each item that was sold; Frattville paid $18,785 for all the items that were sold during the week.
>
> ***7.** Crestway food cost% for the week was 37.55%; their prior week (the week before) food cost % was 37.20%; the company set their food cost target % for Frattville at 38.50%; Crestway is doing well in their food cost %, because their food cost % did not pass the company's set target.
>
> ***8.** Folley food cost % for the week was 37.84%; the company's food cost % target for Folley was 36.60%; Folley went over their food cost % target that the company set for them; this is not good; Folley will have to come up with an action plan that will help them control their inventory better, so they will not go over the company's food cost target % in the future.
>
> ***(9)** Crestway has the most ending Inventory in their store; they had $18,531 of items or product that was remaining in their store after the week period end inventory count.
>
> ***10** English Fort sold the most beverages % within the district; they sold 79.40% beverage for the week.
>
> ***11.** Folley spent $6,648 in payroll dollars for the week.
>
> ***12.** Frattville cashier hours are 115.
>
> ***13.** Crestway server hours are 411.
>
> ***14.** Frattville had the most total hours within the district; their total hours was 1,277.
>
> ***15.** Folley cashier hours is also -11; this means the store was under 71 in cashier hours; which means that the store has 11 more hours to spend on their cashiers; but they didn't use the 11 hours; this also means they saved 11 cashier hours; they could have scheduled 11 more hours for the cashiers.
>
> ***16.** The only store that had overtime hours for the week was Frattville; they also went over in their Other Hours Budget by +11; this means Frattville went over the company's other hour's budget by 11.

*Review the Inventory & Performance Summary Report until you are familiar with the chart. Ask your company about their Inventory & Performance chart, so you can get familiar with their chart.

Let's Review A Cashier's Journal Tape

*When reviewing a cashier's Journal Tape at your business it may be similar to This:

CASHIER (A)		CASHIER (B)	
Chell Jones		Vette Jones	
Cashier # 001		Cashier # 002	
Accessories	$1,500.00	Accessories	$3,000.00
Apparel	$3,500.00	Apparel	$4,400.00
Books	$ 200.00	Books	$ 400.00
Electrical	$ 800.00	Electrical	$1,200.00
Furniture	$2,000.00	Furniture	$2,000.00
Shoes	$ 900.00	Shoes	$ 700.00
Holiday Ornament	$ 300.00	Holiday Ornament	$1,000.00
Charity	$ 50.00	Charity	$ 200.00
Produce	$ 500.00	Produce	$ 650.00
Dairy	$ 537.20	Dairy	$ 400.00
Meat	$ 700.00	Meat	$1,200.00
Wares	$ 300.00	Wares	$ 350.00
Sales Tax	$1,128.72	Sales Tax	$1,550.00
Total Sales	$12,415.92	Total Sales	$17,050.00
Voids	($-70.00)	Voids	($-5.00)
Returns	($-15.00)	Returns	($-0)
Credit Cards	($1,000.00)	Credit Cards	(3,000.00)
Checks	(500.00)	Checks	(1,500.00)
Total Cash Deposit	$10,830.92	Total Cash Deposit	$12,545.00

*NOTE: To get the Total Cash Deposit amount; you have to subtract the voids, returns, credit cards, and the checks away from the total sales amount.

*Remember: Some cashier drawers start out with $200.00 in the drawer. After taking the Total Cash deposit out of the cashier's drawer, $200.00 should be still in the cash drawer.

In reviewing the Cashier's Journal Tape; the Inventory Manager Staff should have a talk with Cashier A, because her voids are $70.00. This is $70.00 that has been rung up as a sale, and then taken off as a mistake of some kind; there should be a written explanation of all voids that are taken off a ticket; if the void is at the customer request; the void should be sign by the customer, cashier, and the manager who conducted the void. **Cashier A** may need some more training on the register. The manager should monitor Cashier A for a couple of days to determine if additional training is needed; this will reduce the amount of voids & mistakes cashier A is making.

All persons who are involved with inventory should review cashiers tape every day to look for voids, returns, and shortages in the journal tape, this will help you keep control of inventory.

(a). If a cashier continues to have a lot of voids or shortages in cash the cashier should get a written notice of this performance; maybe the cashier needs to be moved to another position in the store to see if they can perform better in another position; cashiering may not be for that person.

(b). If the company has a lot of returns and it's because of constant defect in a product, the company should give their suppliers or vendors a call and discuss this problem. Return product will impact a company's revenue.

(c). Shortage in cash will hurt the business revenue and sales. This should be a discussion or possibly disciplinary actions.

LET'S REVIEW THE CASHIER'S JOURNAL TAPE

Total Sales = This is the total dollar amount of items that the cashier sold during their shift.

Voids = This is items that was rung up and sold; but for whatever reason the item or product had to be taken off the receipt, and money was given back to the customer. This is sales that the company had; but then taken away.

Returns = This is an item that was returned to the store, because the customer was not satisfied with the product for some reason (damaged, didn't work, etc.). The customer gets money back for the returned item or they exchange the item for the same item. This impacts the company revenue and sales.

Credit Cards = This is the total dollar amount that the customers paid with credit cards.

Checks = This is the total dollar amount that the customers paid with checks.

Total Cash Deposit = This is the amount of cash that you take out the cashier draw and deposit it at the company's assigned bank.

*(a) Cashier B sold $3,000.00 in Accessories during her shift.
*(b) Cashier A sold $900.00 in shoes during her shift.
*(c) Which cashier sold the most Holiday Ornaments?
    (cashier B) - $1,000.00
*(d) Which cashier sold the less in Meat?
    (cashier A) - $700.00
*(e) Which cashier had more credit cards sales?
    (cashier B) - $3,000.00
*(f) Which cashier had $500.00 in checks?
    (cashier A)

*(g) The total of the company cash deposit for both cashiers' is **$23,375.92**
   Cashier A = $10,830.92 + Cashier B $12,545.00 = $23,375.92

NOTE: Each department in the store can see exactly how much their department made that day; by adding both cashier's journal tapes.

Example: The Shoe Department sold = $1,600.00

Cashier A sold $900.00 in shoes; + Cashier B sold $700.00 in shoes = $1,600.00

Produce Department sold = $1,150.00; Cashier A sold $500.00 in produce + Cashier B sold $650.00 in produce = $1,150.00.

Apparel Department sold = $7900.00; Cashier A sold $3,500.00 in apparel + Cashier B sold $4,400.00 in apparel = $7,900.00.

Meat Department sold = $1,900.00; Cashier A sold $700.00 in meat + Cashier B sold $1,200.00 in meat = $1,900.00.

LET'S REVIEW MORE INVENTORY TRACKING TIPS

1. Make sure all departments are will organized, neat, and properly rotated.
2. Make sure missing inventory is monitored and tracked; and make sure missing product is counted more often to prevent theft of a product.
3. Make sure all items are being sold and not given away at registers and back warehouse.
4. Make sure companies par levels are in place; if not in place the par levels of each items needs to be created immediately.
5. Make sure all invoices received are accurate and entered in the inventory records.
6. Make sure all products received by vendors and suppliers are closely checked it for accuracy in amount, good quality of product, prices are correct, and all invoices has signatures of who check the invoice.
7. Make sure the company has a Waste Sheet or Items Throw Away Sheet to track items that was not useable or not sold due to some type of damage.
8. Make sure you pre-portion most items according to the volume of the business. This mostly applies to business that sells entrees.

Example: If the business use ½ cup of cheese for each garden salad it prepares; and the business usually sells 15 garden salads a day; pre-portion 15 small plastic clear portion bags of ½ cup of cheese. Then when the garden salad are prepared a already portion bag is ready to pour on the garden salad with the correct proper measurements for the cheese. Pre-portioning most items according to the business daily sales will be beneficial and help control the business inventory tremendously.

9. Be very careful when ordering product in bulk prices from suppliers and vendors. Carefully review your inventory records before ordering products by the bulk, because the business might not need to order certain products by the bulk; which

will result in an over stock of inventory and spending money that the business could have saved in the bank.

> **Example:** If the business ordered 1,000 beach balls in a bulk from a vendor for a $10.00 discount price, and the business only sells 300 beach balls a year, according to your inventory report; this means you will have beach balls sitting in your warehouse or stock room taking up unnecessary space for over 2 years before they are sold. The discount was not worth taken, because the business will be stuck with the beach balls for over 2 years.

10. When receiving a shipment from vendors put the date that you received the shipment on the outside of each case with a black magic marker, where it is visible for the staff to see when they look at each case. This is good for keeping the accurate flow of rotation and it also prevent spoilage of a product; and also good for inspections.

11. Using Day Dots is a good tool for controlling inventory; Day Dots are colorful round dots that has each day of the week imprinted on the (Mon-Sun). In the food business some staff members prep items (this is items that are cut, portioned, put away in a container and ready for use) and put items in their assigned department, they put the day dot on the container to show what day and date the item was prepared; they then write the date on the day dot; the day dot will inform everyone of what day and the date the item was prepared. This is good to keep all items in the proper rotation. Items should be prepped each day only according to the business sales.

12. Some business have a choice of holding a lot of back stock in the warehouse or to do ordering more often; the best choice is to order more often instead of ordering a lot of items and let the items sit in the warehouse and having a lot of back stock that is not selling within a inventory time period. When a business have too much back stock in the warehouse that are not moving in a period of time; then the business will have to start selling the items at a discount price; the business is also taken a decrease in revenue on the product; because the product is not being sold at the regular retail price.

13. Most businesses have managers that have keys to open and close its stores; these keys operated all locks within the location. The business should always make sure all keys are accounted for that was issued. If keys are lost the locks should be changed immediately.

14. Set up a schedule to ensure that no one is ever working alone in a store.

15. Providing lockers or a secure place for employees to put their personnel belonging in the store during their shift. Personnel belongings should not be next to a stockroom, working area, or cash registers for any reason, etc.

16. **DO NOT** let employees ring up their own purchases, or ring up their family members at the register for any reason. This will help keep honest people honest.

17. Most business should have a set up for all cash register for a accountability system for anyone operating a register. All daily transactions should be track able to a cashier. This register track able system should be set up to track all paid outs, voids, refunds, etc. When these transactions take place they should be verified by a second party, with the cashier and second party signature.

18. DO NOT leave delivery people unattended in unsecured warehouse areas. Back stock is venerable to theft.
19. All receiving deliveries doors or gates should be closed and locked when not in uses for delivery.
20. A store departments and isles should provide great visibility. If a store is long and narrow, it would be best to run the isles lengthwise instead of across.
21. A lot of lighting in the store will help deter the prospective theft. All areas that are dim, dark and dead ends areas in the store should be turned into bright and noticeable attraction areas.
22. A company that has security mirrors and a alarm system also deter shoplifting. Some alarm systems have codes for employees, which they must register their own personnel code in order to enter the building during off hours without setting off the alarm. This is a great tool for tracking who and when the employee entered the building. This is another way to help keep employees honest.
23. Always check the interior and exterior of the building for each access. Always look for extra security measures; such as: More light inside & outside the back door and receiving area; sometimes its good to have a fence around the loading dock; trash dumpsters free of debris; leave some lights on inside the store after hours, etc.
24. All money should be removed from cash registers at the time of closing the business for the night, and leave the drawers open to deter theft. Bank deposit and receipts should be done every day; sometimes more than one time a day.
25. Always keep inventory fresh, full and rotated at all times
26. Set a time aside daily to review and study all records of you inventory sales. Look for improvement areas, troubled areas (Red Flags), and items that need to be closely monitored daily.
27. Put an Action Plan in place and set a time goal in which your inventory improvements will reflex and show a major difference on the inventory results. When implementing your inventory action plan it should see increasing improvements results within 3 to 4 weeks, sometimes earlier.
28. Make sure employees are scheduled in the right place for the volume of the daily business.

Example: If an employee is unloading new products into the store, but has a consistency of dropping and damaging product every time they unload product; this employee might not be the best fit for unloading products off the truck. This will cost the business a lot in inventory revenue and profits. This employee might be a best fit in another position in the store. You may have to position this employee in a couple of positions to find the best fit for that employee. **This is called putting your aces in the right places.**

Example: If a cashier has a consistency of voids, cash shortages or overage in cash, customers' complaints, etc. This employee might not be the best fit for a cashier. This will cost the business a lot in inventory revenue, sales and profits. This employee might be a best fit in another position in the store. **This is called putting the aces in the right places.**

Example: If a cook consistently burn, drop, or over cook and under cook food; this employee might not be the best fit for a cook. This will impact the food cost and drive your food cost percent (%) to go over the company's budget. (Not Good).

29. Always use your items waste sheet, item return sheet, or damage sheet; whichever one the company uses.
30. Always make sure if the company uses coolers, refrigerators, steamers, freezers, ovens, roasters, etc.; that they all are at the proper temperature. This will reduce a major lost of inventory products. This will also help keep inspections at a high score and keep a healthy environment for workers and customers.
31. Make sure all employees understand how important teamwork, inventory, sales, and profit are to the business. Ensure the employees how important they are as individual in making sure the company's always have a profitable bottom line.
32. Most retail and grocery store should always make sure that all products on the sales floor should always be rotated by the date in which they were received.
33. A inventory person should never pad the inventory numbers for any reason; this means DO NOT report false numbers on a inventory report, or add items to the inventory count that are not really there. If an item is not in the store, and its missing from inventory; the company should just take the lost and make a action plan to make sure the missing items will be monitored more closely to prevent having missing items. Reporting false numbers will sometimes result in immediately termination.
34. A inventory person should always make sure that if they start writing off items from inventory; they need to have a very good reason that is acceptable; such as (discontinued items that need to be slowly dropped from inventory) etc.
35. Make sure you monitor and count all products that are delivered by truck drivers; sometimes truck drivers who delivers to a business will forget to take all the items off the truck; and sometimes they leave items on the truck intentionally; this is free product for them to take for themselves; this is not what we would like to think is possible; but unfortunately it happens far too often.

PART 6

LET'S TALK PAYROLL BUDGET

Inventory sales and payroll budgets work hand in hand. You need enough workers each day to keep up with the sales volume of a store. The more inventories a business sell, the more employees the business need to operate the store to continue to keep up with high volume sales. You need fewer employees for a low volume store.

Payroll needs to be precise and payroll is an important part of a company's operation. The federal and state government requires employers to comply with wages and hourly standards to ensure that employees are paid accurately and on time. The Internal Revenue Service (IRS) and the State Department of Revenue have employment tax requirement that employers must comply with. These factors play an important role in why payroll should be precise.

The U.S Department of Labor, Wage and Hour Division, oversees federal labor laws, and the state department of labor administers the state labor laws. Regulations include the following conditions under which an employee can be classified as non-exempt or exempt employee, minimum paydays that an employee should receive their payment by, employee's final paycheck criteria, employee's meal and rest period requirements, wage garnishment application and permissible deductions that can be made from employees' paychecks. Failure to comply with hour and wage laws can result in a company paying the employee back wages, waiting time penalty, liquidated damages, and attorney or court fees, and also the company can face civil and criminal penalties from the federal or state government.

PAYROLL DOLLAR BUDGET = This is very important to many companies. This is the amount of money that the company projects to spend on payroll within a certain time period; (weekly, monthly, and yearly).

The company sets a payroll dollar budget by the sales that the company projected to make within a certain time period. Most companies sometimes set their payroll dollar budget between 33% and 39% of their projected sales within a certain time period.

Meeting a company's expectation for the payroll budget they set for a certain time period is very healthy for the company's revenue and the company's bottom line results. It is always good to be a little under the payroll budget at the end of the time period. This will save the company a little more money in the bank.

Remember Don't be too much under the payroll budget; this can effect and slow down the production and productivity of the business; and can result in poor customer service; and this can decline the company's sales.

Make sure when you budgeting the payroll and making an employee schedule; make sure that all your aces are in the right places and position at the right time on the schedule; this is for the best production and service for the customer's from the time the business opens until the time the business close. Make sure that schedule is within the payroll dollar budget amount. The more cross trained employee's (employees who knows how to work at least 2 or more stations or positions) are the better a company and execute good production and customer service. This also opens more doors for a company to promote their employees within the company.

EXAMPLE
PAYROLL BUDGET PLAN CHART
FY (FACIAL YEAR) 2014 BUDGET

MONTH	SALES	LABOR	LABOR%	GROSS PROFIT
OCTOBER	$95,403	$32,437	34.00%	$62,965
NOVEMBER	$75,850	$29,582	39.00%	$46,268
DECEMBER	$93,900	$36,621	39.00%	$57,279
JANUARY	$102,000	$34,680	34.00%	$67,320
FEBURARY	$85,000	$28,900	34.00%	$56,100
MARCH	$83,000	$27,390	33.00%	$55,610

When a **MASTER BUDGET** is complete and everyone in the Executive Staff signs off on the budget, the format is similar to the chart above. This chart is an example of a 2014 Budget Plan for October-March a store. This charts shows the sales, labor, labor% and gross profit budget for 6 months. Each category is the goals that the company expects the store to reach each month.

All managers within a company and their departments are expected to meet all company budget goals. It is more profit if all departments and units exceed all budget plans in which the company sets.

OCTOBER = The budget sales the store is expected to earn is $95,403; the budget labor dollar the store is expected to only spend is $32,437; the labor % budget is 34.00% of the store sales. This means that the store is allowed to spend only 34.00% of the budget sales on labor (payroll); gross profit is the gross dollar amount ($62,965) that the store is expected to profit after paying for payroll for the month of October.

How To Budget a Labor (Payroll) schedule = October budget labor dollar is $32,437; **Divide $32,437 into 4 (there are 4 weeks in October); this will equal $8,109;** this is the weekly labor budget that the store can spend each week.

Example of Employees Payroll Rates and A Schedule

You must look at the payroll records to see each employee and manager hourly pay rate. If the managers are included in the employee's payroll you should use the managers pay rate also. This helps you when you are preparing the schedule; to help you stay within the company's spending budget for labor.

Note: In order to make a schedule within budget; you will need a payroll hour rate document that might look similar to the following.

NAME	HOURLY RATE	HIRED DATE	VACATION HOURS
Ernest	$8.50	08/15/2011	24
Bushy	$8.00	08/15/2013	10
Rosie	$8.00	08/15/2011	30
Fannie	$8.50	09/14/2011	36
Sam	$8.50	08/15/2012	27
Rita	$8.00	08/15/2011	30
Drek	$8.25	10/03/2012	40
Areree	$8.00	08/15/2011	10
Gloria	$8.00	08/15/2011	15
Reggie	$9.00	09/01/2012	30
Thelma	$8.50	10/01/2011	18
Mike	$7.50	09/20/2012	35
Charles	$9.00	10/05/2013	40
Chelle	$8.50	08/15/2011	40
Sandreka	$8.75	07/22/2012	24
Willie	$9.00	08/15/2011	36

MANGEMENT TEAM

NAME	HOURLY RATE	HIRED DATE	VACATION HOURS
Lavette	$10.00	08/15/2013	40
Wayne	$9.00	09/15/2013	26
Sidney	$9.00	07/15/2014	35
Robert	$9.00	10/01/2014	31

NOW THAT THE CHART SHOWS EACH EMPLOYEE HOURLY WAGE;

MOST COMPANY'S GIVE THEIR FULL-TIME EMPLOYEES AT LEAST 35 HOURS A WEEK $ MANAGERS USUALLY HAVE AT LEAST 40 HOURS A WEEK!

If each employee works 35 hours a week; this will be their weekly gross dollar amount that the company will spend on each employee:

Example:

EMPLOYEES

Ernest =	$8.50 X 35 =	$297.50
Bushy =	$8.00 X 35=	$280.00
Rosie =	$8.00 X 35=	$280.00
Fannie=	$8.50 X 35=	$297.50

Sam =	$8.50 X 35=	$297.50
Rita =	$8.00 X 35=	$280.00
Drek =	$8.25 X 35=	$288.75
Areree =	$8.00 X 35=	$280.00
Gloria =	$8.00 X 35=	$280.00
Reggie =	$9.00 X 35=	$315.00
Thelma =	$8.50 X 35=	$297.50
Mike =	$7.50 X 35=	$262.50
Charles =	$9.00 X 35=	$315.00
Chelle =	$8.50 X 35=	$297.50
Sandreka =	$8.75 X 35=	$306.25
Willie =	$9.00 X 35 =	$315.00

MANAGEMENT TEAM (Four managers Working 40 hours a week)

Lavette = $12.00 X 40 = $480.00
Wayne = $10.00 X 40 = $400.00
Sidney = $9.00 X 40 = $360.00
Robert = $9.00 X 40 = $360.00

*All employees working 35 hours in one week = $4,690.00

*All managers working 40 hours in one week = $1,600.00

*Total dollar amount spent for all employees added together is = $ 6,290.00

($4,690.00 + $1,600.00 = $6,290.00)

*Remember the company set the labor dollar budget at $32,437 for October (Review Labor Chart); then after dividing 4 into this amount the weekly labor dollar budget was $8,109; the labor dollar amount for all employees is $6,290.00; which means the schedule is under the company's set labor dollar goal. This saved the company $1,819.00 in labor dollars in one week.

($8,109.00 - $6,290.00 = $1,819.00).

TIP If this schedules is used each week for the month of October, the company will save $7,276.00 in labor dollars. ($1,819.00 X 4 weeks = $7,276.00)

The company can use the savings by hiring more employees or giving their excising employees rises.

The following is an example of the schedule of the labor budget that was just discussed: Lunch break and breaks are included in the schedule.

Name	Monday	Tuesday	Wednesday	Thursday	Friday	Saturday	Sunday
Ernest	8a-3:30p	OFF	3:30p-10:30p	OFF	9a-4:30p	9a-4:30p	7:30a-3p
Bushy	3p-10:30p	3p-10:30p	OFF	OFF	8a-3:30p	8a-3:30p	8a-3:30p
Rosie	OFF	OFF	3:30p-11p	7a-2:30p	7a-2:30p	7a-2:30p	7a-2:30p
Fannie	7a-2:30p	3:30p-11p	OFF	OFF	1p-8:30p	1p-8:30p	9a-4:30p
Sam	OFF	OFF	3:30p-11p	7a-2:30p	10a-5:30p	10a-5:30p	7a-3p
Rita	OFF	8a-3:30p	OFF	3p-10:30p	11a-6:30p	11a-6:30p	11a-6:30p
Drek	7a-2:30p	OFF	OFF	7:30a-3p	12p-7:30p	12p-7:30p	12p-7:30p
Areree	9a-4:30p	OFF	3p-10:30p	3:30p-11p	OFF	3:30p-11p	10a-5:30p
Gloria	OFF	9a-4:30p	7a-2:30p	8a-3:30p	OFF	2p-9:30p	7a-2:30p
Reggie	7:30a-3p	11a-6:30p	OFF	7:30a-3p	OFF	11a-6:30p	3:30p-11p
Thelma	11a-6:30p	OFF	7a-2:30p	OFF	3:30p-11p	3:30p-11p	2p-9:30p
Mike	3:30p-11p	OFF	8:30a-4p	OFF	2-9:30p	7a-2:30p	1p-8:30p
Charles	OFF	3:30p-11p	7:30a-3p	OFF	3:30p-11p	7:30a-3p	11a-6:30p
Chelle	3:30p-11p	3:30p-11p	OFF	OFF	3p-10:30p	3p-10:30p	3p-10:30p
Sandreka	OFF	3:30p-11p	8a-3:30p	OFF	3:30p-11p	3:30p-11p	3:30p-11p
Willie	OFF	7:30a-3p	OFF	3:30p-11	3:30p-11p	3:30p-11p	3:30p-11p

MANAGEMENT

Name	Monday	Tuesday	Wednesday	Thursday	Friday	Saturday	Sunday
Lavette	7a-4p	OFF	2p-11p	OFF	7a-4p	7a-4p	8a-5p
Wayne	10a-7p	7a-4p	OFF	2p-11p	OFF	8a-5p	2p-11p
Sidney	2p-11p	OFF	7a-4p	OFF	2p-11p	10a-7p	7a-4p
Robert	OFF	2p-11p	OFF	7a-4p	10a-7p	2p-11p	10a-7p

Note: If any employee take a 30 minutes or 1 hour lunch this schedule will still be within budget.

Review the payroll budget plan chart, employees hourly rate chart, sales budget, labor budget, labor % budget, gross profit, and the budget schedule for all employees until you are familiar with all charts.

PAYROLL'S HOURLY SCHEDULE BUDGET

1. Many companies and business will tell the managers how many hours they are allowed to use each week in the store or in their departments. If your store **Hour Payroll Budget** (how many working hours that are used) is 1,100 hours weekly and you have 3 departments in your store; (Cashier, Server, Other) Divided by () 3 into 1,100 = 366.6. Each department has 366 hours for employees schedule in each department.

EXAMPLE:

Cashier	MON.	TUES.	WED.	THUR.	FRI.	SAT.	SUN.
Sue	8-5	8-5		8-5	2-11		8-5
Pam	2-11	2-11	2-11	2-11			2-11
Lin			8-5	8-5	8-5	8-5	2-11

John		8-5	8-5		2-11	2-11	8-5
Steve	2-11		2-11	2-11	8-5	2-11	

*Total cashier hours = 200

Server

Kim	8-5	8-5		2-11		2-11	8-5
Amy		2-11	2-11		8-5	8-5	2-11
Tod	2-11		8-5	8-5	2-11		2-11

*Total Server hours = 120

Bartender (Other Department)

Bob	11-8	11-8	11-8			2-11	2-11
Rita	2-11	2-11		2-11	11-8	11-8	

*Total Bartender hours = 80

Cook/
Dishwasher (Other Department)

Jack	11-8			11-8	8-5	11-8	11-8
Nancy	12-9	12-9		8-5	11-8		12-9
Kale	8-5	8-5	8-5			2-11	8-5
Jim	2-11	2-11	2-11			8-5	2-11

*Total Cook/Dishwasher hours = 160

*Total Labor Hours for the week spent is 560. Your budget is 1,100; you saved 540 in Labor hours this week.

*You can use this extra 540 hours to bring in more staff for this week; so you can cover more shifts, or hire more people.

*Be careful not to exceed the 540. It is always best to save at least 30 hours a week for emergency overtime hours.

*Carefully make sure you don't go over payroll dollar budget, and don't go over working hour's budget.

PART 7

SOME MAIN KEY'S TO EXECUTING AND EXCEEDING PROFITS IN UNIT'S, REGION'S, DISTRICT'S, AND COMPANIES: AT THE HIGHEST LEVEL OF SUCCESS!!

1. Safe working conditions
2. Have supplies needed
3. Accurate inventory counts executed
4. Making sure all invoices, shipment received & shipped are accurate
5. Profit & Loss are executed
6. Cleanliness of Store
7. Cost control is executed
8. Organization is executed
9. Budget hours/Budget dollar payroll/ Schedules are executed
10. Comfortable expressing concerns w/management
11. Management Confidentiality
12. Understand what's Expected
13. Adequate Feedback
14. Feel Informed
15. Informed about company
16. Receives recognition
17. Like & Enjoy work
18. Moving up
19. Aware of promotions
20. Better Job = Better Chance
21. Management Availability
22. Confidence in management
23. Morale
24. Supervisor Support
25. Use all measuring utensils when required
26. Employee/MGMT. relationship
27. NO Gossip
28. MGMT. Consistency & Fairness
29. Team Cooperation
30. Confidence in Division Leadership
31. Confidence in Senior Leadership
32. Adequate Training
33. Opportunity to Improve
34. Link to Mission
35. Fair Share
36. Feel Valuable
37. Treated with respect

Paying off Debt = Paying off Debt is very good for a company; this tells you that the company is doing well and is in a good financial position.

Recognizing the Special Line Items = A company use this line for any discontinuation of an operation. This line is also used for companies that have international operations. When companies have international operations this relates to **exchanging cash** within different countries; this is called **Foreign Exchange.**

Foreign Currency Exchange = When a company has global operations, they are sure to have a cost for moving money from one country to another country. The U.S dollar and the other countries dollars have currency exchange rates. These rates changes more than 85 times a day.

The Right Credit Policy For Companies Is Very Important

*The Account Receivable Policy can have a major impact on the company's sales. The company must set the right account receivable policy for the company to see an increase in sales.

1. **Some Company's Policy Can Be Too Strict :**
(a)   A company may require customers to pay within 8 days after their billing date or the company will close the customer's account.
(b)   A company that requires its customers to have a very high salary level in order to qualify to have an account with the company.

*Many customers will be forced to go to another company to buy the products they need and get an account with another company, because the company policy is just too strict.

1. **Some Company's Policy Can be Too Loose:**
(a)   A company may have a policy that gives their customers 55 days to pay their accounts.

*This can take the company longer to realize that their customers are not paying their bill. By the time the company realizes this; their customers may be very behind in paying their bill and have a large amount (owe an outstanding amount) of money they owe to the company.

*If the customer never pays the amount due, the company has to write it off as a **Bad Debt**. The company will then take a lost in revenue and a lost in product.

Let's Calculating Accounts Payable Ratio: (This tells how quickly a company pays its bills)

a.   Divide ( ) the cost of goods sold (you will find this figure on the income statement) by the average accounts payable (you will find this figure on the balance sheet). **Example (Store CD)**

1.   Find the average accounts payable:
a.   **$445,753,000** (2013 = Accounts Payable) + **$497,557,000** (2014 = Account Payable)=**$943,310,000**; then **Divided $943,310,000** by 2 = **$471,655,000** (Average Accounts payable)

Use that number to calculate accounts payable turnover ratio:

    a.   **$4,115,795** (cost of goods sold); then Divide **by $471,655,000** (Average accounts payable) = **8.7** times per year.

EXAMPLE: 2 (STORE BC)

    1. **Finding the average accounts payable:**
    a.   **$144,975,000** (2013 = Accounts payable) + **$149,710,000** (2014 = Accounts payable) = **$294,685,000** ; then **Divided $294,685,000** by 2 = **$147,342,500** (Average account payable)

    2. **Use that number to calculate accounts payable turnover ratio:**
    a.   **$1,763,860,000** (cost of goods sold); then **Divided by $147,342,500** (Average accounts payable) = **12.0** times per year.

*****(Store BC)** turns over its accounts payable faster than (Store CD). Store BC pays its Accounts Payable 12 times a year; which means this store pays their bill once a month.

Store CD pays its Accounts Payable bills 8.7 times a year; which means 4 months almost 5 months out of a year they don't pay their bills on time.

*When the company's accounts payable turnover ratio is high; this means the company is paying their bills on time each month.

*When a company's accounts payable turnover ratio is low; this may means the company is having a cash flow problem.

The Number of Days In Accounts Payable Ratio = This will show the number of days it takes the company to pay its bills.

Let's Calculate The Ratio:

    1. Average accounts payable **(Divided by)** Cost of goods sold; **then** (times) **(X) 360 days** = Days in accounts payable
    2. Company's use 360 days for a year; the full calendar year is 365 days; company's base each month on a 30 day month only. (30 X 12 = 360)

Example:

Store CD = **$471,655,000** (Average accounts payable) **(Divided by)** **$4,115,795** (cost of goods sold) **X 360** (Days in Year) = **41.3 days.**

*****Store CD**= CD pays its bills most likely every 41.3 days; which means the company pays its bill about every 5 ½ weeks.

* If Store CD pays its bills every 5 ½ ; and its customers don't pay their bill to the company but every 9 weeks; this means that the company is receiving cash from its customers at

a slower pace than the company is paying their bills. This can lead the company to have cash flow problems.

Store BC = $147,342,000 (Average accounts payable) **(Divided by)** $1,763,860,000 (Cost of goods sold) **X 360** (Days in Year) = **30.1 days**

*Store BC = BC pays its bills most likely every 30.1 days; which means the company pays its bill monthly.

*If Store BC pays its bills every month; if store BC is paying their bills more quickly than its customers are paying their bills, this could also lead to a cash flow problem. This is why company's need to make sure that the customers is paying their bills on time.

REVIEWING INVENTORY & STATEMENT REPORTS

INVENTORY = Any products a company holds ready for sale.

INVENTORY ON THE BALANCE SHEET = This is the cost that the company paid for its items or product; not the price the company will sell the product or item for.

*LET'S TALK (FIFO)

> ***1. First In, First Out (FIFO)** = This is a system that the oldest items or products are sold first, and company's use this when they are concerned about **spoilage or discontinued items.**
> > a. Food stores use FIFO because most items have expiration dates; the item will lose quality in a short period of time; first in, first out items needs to be sold quickly, this will prevent items from sitting on the shelves too long to spoil.
> > b. Computer company's use first in, first out because their products become outdated quickly. The older products need to be sold first.
> > c. **FIFO** = FIFO makes the bottom line look better and FIFO will increase the company's net profit from sales.
>
> ***2. Last In, First Out (LIFO)** = This is a system in which the newest inventory is sold first. Companies use this for products or items that don't spoil. The products or items that come in last and the most expensive should be sold first.

*LIFO = This Increases the company's cost of good value; because it lowers the company's net income from sales and it will decrease a company's tax liability. Hardware stores that sell hammers, nails, screws, and other items that are always the same each year and won't spoil are good examples of LIFO.

Average Costing = This is the accurate cost of what the company paid for its inventory. This gives the company a good knowledge of the company's inventory's cost trends. The company is able to budget inventory dollars from this cost trend.

*When a company receives each new shipment of inventory, it calculates an average cost for each product by adding in the new inventory.

*A company that consistently receives inventory products or items that the prices go up and down often; the average cost of each item can level out the unbalance prices of the inventory cost throughout the year. This will balance the cost of the company's inventory dollars spent. Most Gas station companies use the average costing system a lot.

Specific Identification = This system tracks the actual cost of each individual piece of inventory. Companies that sell very expensive items such as; cars use this system; they use this system due to each one of the items has a difference in accessories:

Example: Most cars have different accessories inside; one car may have expensive rims, one car may not; one car may have a CD surround system, one car may not; one car may have had an upgrade; one car may not; this is why the company uses the specific identification system. Each car that comes onto the company's lot has different set of features, so this will make the prices different for each car. This is also the same for high-end computers.

(LCM) LOWER OF COST OR MARKET = This system sets the value of

Inventory based on the lowest cost the company paid –this is the actual cost of the products on hand or the current market value of the product. Companies that sell products that fluctuate consistently use this system.

*Studying how well a company manages its assets is a critical step in measuring how effectively the company uses its resources; this is very important to review.

*There are so many factors that directly impact the company's cost of selling a product, including producing the product, purchasing the products or the materials that are not produced in-house, storing the products in the stock room or warehouse until it's sold, and shipping the product to the customer or store where the product is sold. If a company doesn't sell its product fast enough, the product may become discontinued or damaged before it's sold; this can be a lost in the company's revenue.

***Let Us Review** the measures you can use to gauge how well a company manages its assets, especially its inventory, and how quickly the company sells the inventory.

*Inventory is very important to the company's bottom line. The reason is that the numbers the company uses on its income statement report for their cost of goods sold depends on the cost the company assigns for each product in inventory it sold during the period that the **Income Statement** covers.

***ENDING INVENTORY'S VALUE** = This is the value of the goods that the company still holds (remaining in the store). You can also find the inventory's value on the **Balance Sheet**. This is the value of what's left over and still held by the company.

***BEGINNING INVENTORY** = This is the number that's used at the beginning of the next accounting period; any purchases that the company made during this period are added onto the beginning inventory.

REVIEW THE FORMULA FOR CALCULATING THE COST OF GOODS SOLD

1. Find the value of the goods available for sales
   Beginning Inventory + Purchases = Goods Available For Sale
2. Calculate the value of items sold
   Goods available for sale – Ending Inventory = Value of Items Sold

3 METHODS ARE: AVERAGE COSTING/FIFO/LIFO = These 3 methods will show you how to go through the formula and calculations for the cost of goods value.

(a).   AVERAGE COSTING, (b). FIFO, (c). LIFO

- 300 is the (Beginning Inventory) + 500 (items that were Purchase) = 800 (Goods available for sale)
- 800 is the (Goods available for sale) – 300 (Ending Inventory) = 500 (Items sold)

* The company had 3 inventory purchases during the month of September:

September 5th	100	at	**$11.00**
September 12th	200	at	**$12.00**
September 22 nd	200	at	**$13.00**

*The beginning inventory value was 300 items at $8.00 each= $2,400

AVERAGE COSTING = Calculating the average cost per product; **Example**

300 at $8.00 = $2,400.00 (Beginning Inventory)

Plus Purchases:

100	at	$11.00	=	$1,100	(September 5th Purchase)
200	at	$12.00	=	$2,400	(September 12th Purchase)
200	at	$13.00	=	$2,600	(September 22nd Purchase)

*Cost of goods available for sale = $8,500

Average Cost Per Unit = $8,500 (Cost of goods available for sale) Divided by ( ) 800 (Number of units) = $10.63 (Average cost per unit)

*When you know the average cost per unit, you can calculate the cost of goods sold and the ending inventory value pretty easily by using the average costing inventory system: **Example:**

Cost of goods sold	500	at	$10.63 each	=	$5,315
Ending Inventory	300	at	$10.63 each	=	$3,189

*The value of cost of goods sold using the average costing method is $5,315. This figure is the one you see as the **Cost of goods sold** line item on the **income statement**.

*The value of inventory left on hand, or **Ending Inventory**, is **$3,189**. This number will be on the balance sheet; most likely called the inventory item.

FIFO

*To calculate FIFO, you don't average costs. Instead, you look at the costs of the first units the company sold. FIFO= the first units sold are the first units put on the shelves. Beginning inventory is sold first; then the next set of purchases; then you continue this rotation.

*To find the cost of goods sold, add the beginning inventory to the purchases made during the reporting period. The remaining 200 units at $13.00 are the value of **Ending Inventory.** (Here's The Calculation)

Beginning Inventory:	300	at $8.00	= $2,400
September 5th Purchase	100	at $11.00	= $1,100
September 12th Purchase	200	at $12.00	= $2,400
September 22nd Purchase	200	at $13.00	= $2,600

Cost of goods sold = $8,500

Ending Inventory

From March 25th : 200 at $13.00 = $2,600

*In this example, the cost of goods sold includes the value of the beginning inventory plus the purchases on September 5th and 12th and part of the purchase on September 22nd. The units that remain on the shelf are from the purchase on September 22nd. The cost of goods sold is $8,500, and the value of the inventory on hand, or the ending inventory, is $2,600.

LIFO

*To calculate LIFO, start with the last units purchased and work backward to compute the cost of goods sold.

The first 300 units at $8.00 in the beginning inventory end up being the same 300 at $8.00 for the ending inventory. (Here's the calculation)

September 22nd Purchase	200	at	$13.00	=$2,600
September 12th Purchase	200	at	$12.00	=$2,400
September 5th Purchase	100	at	$11.00	=$1,100

Cost of goods sold =$6,100

Ending Inventory:
From Beginning Inventory: 300 at $ 8.00 =$2,400.00

*The cost of goods sold line item that you find on the **Income Statement** is $6,100, and the Value of the Inventory line item on the **Balance Sheet** is $2,400.

Inventory Turnover

* Many Companies want to know how quickly it sells its inventory and turns a profit. Companies that turns over its inventory quickly, most likely will not have out dated products sitting on the shelves. Companies that inventory moves slowly will most likely find problem in their inventory system and procedures.

Calculating Inventory turnover = Is a (3) step process to find out how quickly inventory is moving. **Example:**

1. Calculate the average inventory (the average number of units held in inventory).

Beginning Inventory + Ending Inventory (Divided () by 2 = Average Inventory

2. Calculate the inventory turnover (the number of times inventory is completely sold out during the accounting period).

Cost of goods sold (Divided () by Average Inventory = Inventory Turnover

3. Calculate the number of days it takes for products to go through the inventory system, according to the accounting policies in the notes to the financial statement.

365 (Divided () by) Inventory turnover = Number of days to sell all inventory

* **JAZZY STORE 2014 Income Statements and Balance Sheets** to show how to calculate inventory turnover and the number of days it takes to sell its inventory.

This company uses FIFO methods.

1. **Find the average inventory : Example**

*Use the inventory on hand for December 31, 2013, as the beginning inventory, and use the inventory remaining on December 31, 2014, as the ending inventory.

$148,000 (Beginning Inventory) + $146,000 (Ending Inventory) Divided ()

By 2 = $147,000 (Average Inventory).

1. **Calculate the inventory turnover: Example**

*You need the cost of goods sold figure on the 2014 **Income Statement** to calculate the inventory turnover.

$980,970.00 (Cost of goods sold) Divided () by $147,000(Average Inventory) = 6.67 (Inventory turnover)

*This figure means that (**Jazzy Store**) completely sold out its inventory 6.67 times

2. **Find the number of days it took (Toy Store A) to sell out all its inventory:**

365 (Days) Divided () by 6.67 (Inventory Turnover) = 54.7

*This roughly shows that, on average, **Jazzy Store** sells its entire inventory on hand every 54.7 days. Popular items in the Jazzy store may sell out, and new stock may be needed every month. There are also less popular items that may sit on the shelf for several months or more. This calculation gives an average for all types of items sold in the Jazzy store.

JAZZY OUTLET

STATEMENT OF FINANCIAL POSITION   **(Example of a Financial Report)**
(AT, DECEMBER 31ST)

ASSETS	2013	2014
Cash and Equivalents	$56,245	$65,000
Investment Securities	$29,423	$27,000
Current Receivables	$13,431	$12,000
Inventories	$10,400	$12,000
Financing Receivables – net	$100,000	$120,000
Other Jazzy Outlet Receivables	$5,400	$5,000
Property, Plant and Equipment – net	$45,000	$45,000
Investment in Jazzy Outlet	-	-
Goodwill	-	-
Other Intangible Asset – net	$5,000	$6,000
All other Assets	$80,000	$90,000
Assets of Businesses held for Sale	-	-
Assets of Discontinued Operations	-	-
Total Assets	**$344,899**	**$382,000**

Liabilities and Equity

	2013	2014
Short-Term Borrowings	$66,400	$104,350
Accounts payable, principally trade accounts	$11,000	$12,000
Progress collections & price adjustments accrued	$8,000	$9,000
Dividends Payable	$800	$600
Other Jazzy Outlet Current liabilities	$10,000	$9,000

NON- Recourse borrowing of

Consolidated securitization entities	$10,000	$9,000
Bank Deposits	$22,000	$19,000
Long-Term borrowings	$90,000	$97,000
Annuity benefits	$17,000	$18,000
All other liabilities	$43,000	$45,000
Deferred income taxes	($50)	($100)
Liabilities of businesses held for sale	-	-
Liabilities of discontinued operations	-	-
Total Liabilities	**$278,150**	**$322,850**
ASSETS	**2013**	**2014**
Common Stock	$500	$500
Investment Securities	$400	$400
Currency translation adjustments	$200	$50
Cash flow hedges	($500)	($900)
Benefit plans	($17,000)	($19,000)
Other capital	$10,000	$10,500
Retained earnings	$80,000	$73,000
Less common stock held in treasury	($9,851)	($6,000)
Total Jazzy Outlet Shareowners' equity	**$63,749**	**$58,550**
NON Controlling Interests	$3,000	$600
Total Equity	**$66,749**	**$59,150**
Total Liabilities and Equity	**$344,899**	**$382,000**

REVENUES AND

OTHER INCOME	**2014**	**2013**	**2012**
Sales of goods	$55,000	$48,000	$42,000
Sales of services	$10,000	$10,200	$15,000
Other income	$1,000	$4,000	$500
Jazzy Outlet earnings from Continuing operations	-	-	-
Jazzy Outlet revenue from			

Services	$33,099	$32,000	$25,000
Total revenues and other			
Income	**$99,099**	**$94,200**	**$82,500**
Costs and Expenses			
Cost of goods sold	$45,000	$40,000	$35,000
Cost of services sold	$6,000	$5,000	$13,000
Interest and other financial Charges	$1,000	$3,000	$4,000
Investment contracts, Insurance losses and insurance Annuity benefits	$200	$300	$700
Provision for losses on Financing receivables	$1,200	$1,300	$4,000
Other costs and expenses	$19,000	$20,000	$21,000
Total costs and expenses	**$72,400**	**$69,600**	**$77,700**
Earnings from continuing			
Operations before Income Tax	$1,000	$3,000	$800
Benefit for income tax	($100)	($400)	($50)
Earnings from continuing Operation	$900	$2,600	$750

REVENUES AND

OTHER INCOME	2014	2013	2012
Earnings (loss) from Discontinued operations, Net of taxes	-	-	-
Net earnings	$850	$900	$700
Less net earnings attributable To non controlling interests	$20	$40	$200
Less net earnings attributable To the company	$800	$770	$500
Preferred stock dividends Declared	-	-	($600)
Net earnings attributable To Jazzy Outlet common Shareowners	$700	$720	$650

AMOUNTS ATTRIBUTABLE TO THE COMPANY

	2014	2013	2012
Earning from continuing Operations	$1,500	$1,400	$1,000
Earning (loss) from discontinued Operations, net of taxes - - -			
Net earnings attributable			
to the company	**$1,500**	**$1,400**	**$1,000**

PART 8

BUDGETING

*You can find how well a company is doing by comparing the actual numbers with the company's expectations. A company or business hopes to meet its budget targets each week, month, and year. The projected budget can be located on summary reports and financial report; this will show the company's financial needs. Managers will closely reviews and monitor these budget reports to determine how close the company is to meeting its projected budget. When managers recognize they are not meeting company's budget goals, they will quickly try to fix this problem as soon as possible. Managers will put together an action plan throughout the year to make sure the company is meeting its budgeting goals. The Chief Executive Staff and Managers are many times disappointed when the company doesn't reach its budgeting goals.

*A company will set its budget by carefully calculating the amount of revenue it expects from the sales of products and services. The company will carefully budget and calculate the cost of its expenses such as: purchasing the products it sells; and the manufacturing of the products it sell; and other expenses it takes to operate the company.

*Two different approaches companies and businesses use to set budgets.

> ***a.** **Top Down Approach** = Key Executives set budgets and give the budgets to department managers to meet the company's goal. Most employees aren't involved in the budgeting process. Executives will impose the numbers on the management team; and the management team is expected to meet all goals set by the key Executives. Top down approach usually causes problems, because employees frequently complain that the company's budget is very unrealistic.
>
> ***b.** **Bottom-up Approach** = This approach encourages many employees to participate in the budgeting process. When employees are involved in the budgeting process they can't complain about the company's budget; because they helped create the budget.
>
> ***c.** Most managers and staff members like the **Bottom-Up Approach,** because they were involved in creating the budget. The managers also feel more confident that they can meet all the company's expectations within the budget.

GOALS FOR CREATING THE BUDGET

A company must gather information about where the company stands financially before the company set budget goals. They must have information about its surrounding competitors. Then the company will review its financial needs and determine the company's budget goals for the company's best profit.

*The first critical step for goal setting is to develop a **Sales Forecast**

(A projection of the number of sales the company will make during the year).

These factors must be considered to develop an accurate sales forecast.

*Past Sales Success = A company or business will look at the sales by product or service for the past three to five years. A company will look for trends and make the best decision for its future sales growth.

*Potential Pricing Policy = A company will look at its past sales and determine whether its current pricing policy is suitable or whether the company needs to change its pricing policy. Products that are moving slowly off the shelves may need a price cut to boost its sales. Products that are moving very quickly off the shelves may need a price increase.

*Data On Unfilled Orders and Backlogs = This data helps a company determine which product line or services it may need to upgrade or change to meet customers' demands and revenue profit.

*Information About General Economic Conditions = This research gives the budget committee an overview of expected economic conditions for the next year so it knows whether there's potential for growth or a possible reduction in sales. A company can get information from economists predicting a market to be strong or to recover within the economy.

*Industry Economic Conditions = A company closely monitors industry and economic conditions to determine whether the city, state, community, etc. in which it operates is set for growth, or a down fall, or is the company expected to perform at the same level. Many companies monitor, view, and gather information about what's actually happening inside their stores. Many companies will get reports from their employees about how their customers are being treated, contractors, vendors, etc.

How to Build Budgets

(a)*Sales Budget= The companies usually set the sales budget first; because other budgets depends on the sales goal. Many companies will get a sales goal according to previous year sales. Purchasing Managers need a sales budget; this helps them know how many products to buy. Production Managers need a sales budget; this will helps them know how many products to produce.

(b)*Production Budget= A company that manufactures its own product, will create the production budget after the sales budget is completed. The Executive Staff and the Production Manager will look at the beginning inventory that is left from the previous planning period and they will plan what additional inventory is needed for production in the current planning period.

(c)*Inventory Purchases Budget= Many companies don't manufacture their own products; so the company will focus on its purchasing needs.

(d)*Direct Material Budget= The company will budget enough raw materials to make sure production line will move with a constant flow. A company doesn't want to run out of raw materials; because this can cause the company a decrease in profit and revenue.

(e)*Direct Labor Budget= Companies will work hard to make sure they have enough employees to meet its production needs. If a company doesn't have enough employees to meet production needs they will pay a huge amount of money in overtime hours to employees. If the company has too many employees they will spend more money than necessary.

(f)*Selling and Administrative Expense Budgets= This budget is for human resources, accounting, marketing, and finance.

(g)*Master Budget= The accounting department will prepare the Master Budget after the Executive Staff has signed off on the entire budget plan for the company.

(h)*Cash Budget= The accounting department will create a Cash Budget after they complete the Master Budget. The finance department will estimate how much cash the company will need for its operation. The Cash Budget will estimate how much cash the company need monthly.

PART 9

SOME COMPANIES AND MANAGERS WILL PLAY GAMES WITH NUMBERS

*Companies and managers face a lot of pressure meeting monthly and quarterly budget goals. Sometimes companies and managers will play with the numbers trying to meet expectations, which leads to fraud and deception.

*There are laws that were put in place by Congress for companies and businesses. These laws protect investors and customers from misleading accounting practices. These laws help correct the fraud and flaws in the U.S. financial reporting system. Many companies think the laws are a burden to its company; but the laws have removed and lot of fraud and flaws out of many companies.

*Some company's staff members used the corporate accounts for their personal purposes. They will take luxury trips; buy huge houses; buy a couple of condos; and buy expensive cars. This money should be used for growing the company's revenue and profits; but instead they are spending the money for themselves. Many corporate staff members and executive staff members can get away with this, because they are close friends or relatives; and most family members and best friends don't question each other about the company's money they are spending.

*Some staff members within the company will overstate the company's financial position; undervalue their liabilities; and sometimes overvalue the company's assets. Sometime they will take extreme measures to deceive the public. Many times the public will not know about this until an insider blows the whistle.

*Executives and Managers will play games with the numbers because they want to maintain their bonuses; or they don't want to face the reality that the company financial position is poor. Some companies will report pure fiction when reporting sales results.

* If there are major increases and decreases from one accounting period to another accounting period; this may be a sign of trouble. If a company is playing games with its numbers, you can most likely find the evidence in the amortization policies or capitalization in the financial report.

*Getting to the bottom of false financial reports and other false numbers is like playing detective. Any discrepancies that are in reports can be found if you carefully read and analyze these reports.

*Some companies will play games with these expenses: patents and licenses, restructuring charges, advertising, asset impairments, and research and development. Many times they will spread out the cost of these expenses over a number of months, quarters, or years. This helps keep more revenue in their bank. When you are trying to find out if a company is spreading out their expenses properly or improperly it's difficult to do with using the annual report if you are an outsider. The outsider will have to find this information from the SEC, or on reports in the financial press. Sometimes a person working on the inside will blow the whistle eventually.

Some companies will use the Restructuring Charges to hide accounting games that are being played. They will have one division split off into two or more companies, eliminate an entire division, or restructure itself by combining divisions. When a company restructure the business this is a good way to get rid of all the company's losses.

*Many companies will overstate the inventory physical count; so they can improve the balance sheets. They will leave damaged products in the inventory count, even when the products don't have value.

SOME SIGNS THAT A COMPANY IS IN FINANCIAL TROUBLE

1. A company that doesn't have the cash to pay its bills. The company's cash flow statement will show if the company's cash situation is in trouble.
2. If a company's profit margin is dropping year to year; this is a sign of trouble.
3. When a company is reporting false earnings.
4. When a company is borrowing too much money to continue its operations. Many times the company's interest rates will start rising.
5. Too much debt will eventually put the company in bankruptcy.
6. A company that changes its inventory constantly will impact the company's bottom line.
7. When a company's inventory is slowing down; and it become harder to move products off the shelf. When a company's inventory turnover is slowing down this is a sign of trouble.

TIPS ON ENCOURAGING OTHERS AT WORK

*The most frequent question managers ask is how to motivate employees. Many people think they need a high profile structure to get employees to produce good productions, or to get employees to do their jobs to a successful level. Many people typically think money is the key.

*Cash is a good motivator, but constant encouragement does more to motivate employees than money. With constant encouragement companies and business will retain their employees for longer periods of time. This will also lead to the company's significant organizational improvements.

*Employees will respond with more positive work ethic when you provide them with encouragement for a job well done. You will get more positive feedback from your employees. This is a great way to acknowledge that you value your employees; and that they play a major role in your success. Encouraging employees is something many managers don't do often enough within their company or business.

*Employees will thrive more in companies where they feel valued and honored. A few words of encouragement each day to your employees will highly boost the morale in a company.

*Many managers feel they shouldn't have to tell employees they're doing a good job, because that's what the employees are getting paid to do anyway. These are the same managers who most likely have many performance problems with their employees. These types of managers will take immediate action toward their employees to rectify this problem; but many times this situation will keep arriving because of how the employees are being managed. If the employees don't feel valued the company will not be effective; and you will not get the highest revenue and profits out of your employees this way. A simple "Thank You" will go a long way with employees.

*Encouraging your employees also means challenging them for growth and new ideas for solutions to grow the business. Encouraging employees will truly empower your employees to be beneficial to the company; this will make the staff more successful.

*Managers and Executive Staff should make sure they form a habit and perform encouragement inside their company; because the value and power of encouragement will bring the company to a higher success with record breaking increasing revenue and profits.

*Managers and Executive Staff should always find ways to encourage employees' everyday; instead of discouraging employees every day. Encouragement goes straight to the heart of your employees. When the going gets tough and the day feels long, a word of encouragement will pull the staff through rough days and times.

*Managers should always think about what encourages them, and then they should do the same thing for their employees. Managers should always learn their employees this will make the employees feel valued. All employees don't have the same personalities; so learning each employee will be a great tool for the company's success.

*When encouraging thoughts comes to your mind, it should be shared with the employees. Always add a few words of praise to your employees; this will also go a long way with employees; and be specific when you offer words of praise such as: "Great job Rita"; "I really appreciated your hard work today"; "I'm really impressed with how you help our customers"; "Thanks for the great teamwork today", "Great job everyone", etc.

*Managers should make sure that celebrations for the staff's great performance are part of their victories. Make sure you high-five your employees during their good performance.

*Managers should work alongside their employees more often; this makes the employees feel they are important; and being there for your employees is encouraging for your employees as well.

*Managers in the work field many times forget the most important part of communication; and that's listening to their employees. This will go a long way!

*When employees make a positive change in their performance be sure to give them a word of encouragement.

TEAM MEETINGS WITH EMPLOYEES ARE VERY EFFECTIVE

*1. Managers should set a different date and time for each team meetings; this will keep the employees interested and alert during the meetings. Manager should alternate days of the week; and mornings and afternoons for their team meetings. When managers make their team meetings more unusual, the more likely the team will prepare for the meetings.

*2. Managers should make sure that their agenda for team meetings is covering Action Plans for the day, or for the week, or for the month. This will help all employees know the expectations and budget goals that they need to meet.

*3. Managers should always have an Action Plan and information in place and prepared before the team meetings. Having reports, documents, and company's results, and thoughts ahead of time will lead an effective meeting.

*4. Managers should always inform their employees that a great business relationship are created when employees can count on each other to do their part, meet commitments, and get the job done. Employees don't have to like each other, but they do have to work well and execute the business together.

*5. During successful team meetings managers and employees should have discussions that involve ideas, solutions, and suggestions. Managers must be very professional, but at the same time they can't worry too much about hurt feelings as long as the comments from the manager aren't disrespectful or degrading. Many employees appreciate a controlled, well plan, on-point, and productive meeting. The employees who like to whine will soon realize this is not acceptable.

*6. Managers should always make sure employees know and understand the Action Plan that was discussed during the meeting. Employees must have a good and clear understanding of what was decided at the meeting and what needs to be done. If employees don't have a clear understanding, this means the team meeting was a waste of time and wasn't successful; so this means all the manager did was talk.

*7. Managers should create accountability for the employees. All employees should always know who's responsible for which task that was discussed in the Action plan; and how quickly the task needs to be completed.

*8. Managers should establish responsibilities on each employee, and managers must conduct follow-ups with each employee. Always let the employees know when the Action Plan was performed with progress (encouragement).

REALIZING WORKPLACE VIOLENCE

*There have been thousands of attacks on people in the workplace such as: assaults, sexual assaults, and homicides.

*There are attacks on the company's property such as: property damage and vandalism.

*There is harassment such as: racial or Sexual Harassment, bullying, and stalking.

*There are threats such as: extortion, intimidation, verbal or psychological abuse.

A EMPLOYEE WITH TROUBLING WARNING SIGNS

*Signs of emotional problems

*Blames others for their own problems

*Suspicious thinking or behavior

*Sudden behavior changes

*Alcohol or drug abuse

*Bizarre or obsessive thoughts

*Reacts poorly to criticism

*Sexual or racial harassment of co-workers

*Aggressive behaviors toward authority

*Increasingly aggressive behaviors toward co-workers

*History of making threats against co-workers

*History of poor conduct violations, uncooperativeness, and poor performance

*Anger towards people who disagree with them

SIGNS THAT EMPLOYEE HAS REACHED THE EDGE

*Restless behavior, or agitated gestures *Clenched fists movements

*Rapid breathing with anger *Loud talking, shouting, threatening

TAKE THE SELF HONESTY TEST

This test will grade your ability for a successful career in Inventory. The higher the grade the more successful you will become. This is not an open book test; so please take the test honestly without getting the answers from the book. The more you cheat, the more your success level in inventory will decrease. Please check your answers after the test is completed. The pages for each answer will be listed after the test.

*1. What is a financial Report?

*2. What is Liabilities?

*3. What is Equity?

*4. What is Sales?

*5. What is Cost and Expenses?

*6. What is Profit or Loss?

*7. What is Cash Flow?

*8. What is Double-Entry Accounting?

*9. What are the responsibilities of the SEC?

*10. Which companies are required to report to the SEC? **Circle one (Private or Public)**

*11. What are Quarterly Reports?

*12. What are Annual Reports?

*13. What are companies Assets?

*14. What is a Balance Sheet?

*15. What is Net Income or Loss?

*16. What is Excess of Revenues Over Expenses?

*17. What is Excess of Expenses Over Revenues?

*18. What is a Statement of Cash Flows?

*19. What is Cash-Basis Accounting?

*20. What is Tax Liability Accounting?

*21. Debits & Credits will increase or decrease an account. Which of the following accounts will increase or decrease?

ACCOUNT	DEBIT	CREDITS
Assets (Example)	Increase	Decrease
Liabilities		
Income		
Expenses		

*22. What are Tangible Assets?

*23. What are Current Assets?

*24. What is Long-Term Assets?

*25. What is Capitalized Leases?

*26. What is a Leasehold Improvement?

*27. What is Intellectual Property?

*28. Explain a Private Company;

*29. Explain a Public Company;

*30. What is a Form 8-K?

*31. What is another name for an Annual Report?

*32. What is Management's Discussion and Analysis?

*33. What are four key words a company uses for hidden trouble that maybe inside the company? **(a).**   **(b).**

(c).   **(d).**

*34. What is Pension Plans?

*35. What is Environmental and Product Liabilities?

*36. What is Stock-Based Compensation?

*37. What is Allowance for Doubtful Accounts?

*38. What is the Distribution Systems?

*39. What is Product Improvements?

*40. What is Manufacturing Capacity?

*41. What is Research and Development Projects?

*42. What is Capital Resources?

*43. What is an Auditor's Report?

*44. What is Work performed by a different auditor?

*45. What are Accounting policy changes?

*46. What is Material Uncertainties?

*47. What is Going-Concern Problems?

*48. What is Qualified Opinions?

*49. What is Specific Disclosures?

*50. What is Working Capital?

*51. What is Net Assets?

*52. What is Non-Current Assets?

*53. What is Financial Position Format?

*54. What is Short-Term Borrowings?

*55. What is Current portion of Long-Term Debt?

*56. What is Accounts Payable?

*57. What is Accrued Liabilities?

*58. What is Stock?

*59. What is Common Stock?

*60. What is Preferred Stock?

*61. What is Treasury Stock?

*62. What is Capital?

*63. What is Drawing Account?

*64. What is an Income Statement?

*65. What is Cost Control?

*66. What is Expenses?

*67. What is Cost of Goods Sold?

*68. What is General Office needs?

*69. What are Other Selling Administration Expenses?

*70. What are the four different profits lines in the Multi-Step Format?

*71. What is Gross Profit?

*72. What is Income before Taxes?

*73. What is Volume Discounts?

*74. What are Returns?

*75. What is Allowances?

*76. What is Raw Material?

*77. What is Work-in-Process Inventory?

*78. What is Finished-Goods Inventory?

*79. What is Advertising and Promotion?

*80. What is Royalties?

*81. What is an Inventory Purchases Budget?

*82. What is a sales Budget?

*83. Explain how some company's credit policies can be too loose;

*84. What is Accounts Receivable?

*85. What are five keys to the Investment activities section?

*86. Explain three things you do when you receive an Account Receivable Invoice from a vendor;

*87. What is a Par Level?

*88. What is Total Cash Deposit?

*89. What is a Payroll Budget?

*90. What are ten key's to running and exceeding units, regions, districts, and companies; at the highest level of success?

*(a) _____
*(b) _____
*(c) _____
*(d) _____
*(e) _____
*(f) _____
*(g) _____
*(h) _____
*(i) _____
*(j) _____

*91. What is paying off Debt?

*92. What is Foreign Currency Exchange?

*93. Explain how some companies Credit Policy can be too strict;

*94. What is an Accounts Receivable Aging Schedule?

*95. What are Current Liability Accounts?

*96. What are five signs that a company is in financial trouble?

*97. What is Equity Holding?

*98. What is Organizational Structure?

*99. What are padding and fudging inventory numbers?

*100. What is a Void?

*101. What is Inventory?

*102. What explains Inventory on the Balance Sheet?

*103. What are five different Inventory Methods to track inventory?

*104. What is FIFO? Explain

*105. What is LIFO? Explain

*106. What is Specific Identification?

*107. What is Average Costing?

*108. What is Lower of Cost or Market?

*109. Explain the Ending Inventory's Value?

*110. What is the Beginning Inventory?

*111. What is Inventory Turnover?

*112. What is Bad Debt?

*113. What is Top Down Approach?

*114. What is Bottom Up Approach?

*115. What is Sales Forecast?

*116. What is Hour Payroll Budget?

*117. What is Potential Pricing Policy?

*118. What is Data on Unfilled Orders and Backlogs?

*119. Explain Information about General Economic Conditions?

*120. What is Industry Economic Conditions?

*121. What is Equity Holdings?

*122. What is Cash Equivalents?

*123. What is a Sales Budget?

*124. What is a Production Budget?

*125. What is an Inventory Purchases Budget?

*126. What is a Direct Material Budget?

*127. What is a Direct Labor Budget?

*128. What is a Master Budget?

*129. What is a Cash Budget?

*130. When do companies file a Form 10Q?

*131. Write at least five critical events that should be reported on Form 8-K?

*132. What is Cost Control Problems?

*133. What is Corrective Actions that are Being Taken?

*134. Most companies Count their Inventory by the **pint, quarts,** _____, _____ , _____,_____.

*135. What is a Company's Legal Proceedings?

*136. What is GAAP? and what is the GAAP duties?

*137. Explain six different ways some companies play games with their numbers?

*138. Why do some companies overstate inventory?

*139. What are six ways to encourage others at work?

*140. What are six ways to have an Effective Team Meeting?

*141. If the company's sales are declining what things should the company investigate and check? (Write at least five things)

*142. What is Furniture and Fixtures?

*143. What are Tools, Dies, and Molds?

*144. What is Goodwill?

*145. What is Subsidiaries?

*146. When is the best time to count Inventory?

*147. What is an Order Sheet?

*148. What is Lead Time?

*149. What is a Waste Sheet?

*150. What are three signs that an employee has reached the edge?

SCORES: Each question is 1.5 points + 150 =225 (A perfect score)

225 = A+
224-214 = A
213-203 = B+
202-192 = B
192-181 = C+
180-170 = C

Scores that are below **170,** you should research and carefully review the questions that were marked wrong until you have a clear understand of each question. Then you should retake the test; by doing this it will increase your career to the highest level of success.

Note: Any questions that are market wrong on the test should be research and carefully reviewed.

*You can check your answers to each question by the page # listing next to the number. Example: You can find the answer to **(1).On Page 3**

2. Page 3 / 3. Page 3 / 4. Page 3 / 5. Page 3 / 6. Page 3 / 7. Page 3 / 8. Page 4 / 9. Page 4 / 10. Page 4 / 11. Page 4 / 12. Page 4 / 13. Page 4 / 14. Page 4 / 15. Page 5 / 16. Page 5 / 17. Page 5 / 18. Page 5 / 19. Page 5 / 20. Page 5 / 21. Page 6-7 / 22. Page 8 / 23. Page 8 / 24. Page 8 / 25. Page 8 / 26. Page 8 / 27. Page 9 / 28. Page 9 / 29. Page 9-10 / 31. Page 11 / 32. Page 11/ 33. Page 11-12 / 34. Page 12 / 35 Page 12 / 38. Page 13 / 39. Page 14 / 40. Page 14 / 41. Page 14 / 50. Page 16 / 51. Page 16 / 52. Page 16 / 53. Page 16 / 54. Page 17 / 55. Page 17 / 56. Page 18 / 57. Page 18 / 58. Page 18 / 59. Page 18 / 60. Page 18 / 61. Page 18 / 62. Page 18 / 63. Page 18 / 64. Page 19 / 65. Page 19 / 66. Page 22 / 67. Page 20 / 68. Page 22 / 69. Page 22 / 70. Page 19/ 71. Page 21 / 72. Page 19 / 73. Page 20 / 74. Page 20 / 75. Page 20 / 76. Page 20 / 77. Page 20 / 78. Page 20 / 79. Page 22 / 80. Page 23 / 81. Page 76-77 / 82. Page 43-85 / 83. Page 73-74 / 84. Page 23 / 85. Page 23 / 86. Page 32 / 87. Page 32 / 88. Page 61-62 / 89. Page 66-67 / 90. Page 72-73 / 91. Page 73 / 92. Page 73 / 93. Page 73-74 / 94. Page 25-26 / 95. Page 9-10 / 96. Page 88 / 97. Page 10-11 / 98. Page 10-11/ 99. Page 86-87 / 100. Page 62 / 101. Page 75-76 / 102. Page 75-76 / 103. Page 63-64 / 104. Page 76 / 105. Page 76 / 106. Page 76-77 / 107. Page 76-77 / 108. Page 77 / 109. Page 77 / 110. Page 77 / 111. Page 79-80 / 112. Page 74 / 113. Page 84-85 / 114. Page 84-85 / 115. Page 85-86 / 116. Page 71-72 / 117. Page 85 / 118. Page 85 / 119. Page 85 / 120. Page 85 / 121. Page 10 / 122. Page 5-6 / 123. Page 85 / 124. Page 86 / 125. Page 76-77 / 126. Page 67-68-69 / 127. Page 86 / 128. Page 86 / 129. Page 86 / 130. Page 10 / 131. Page 10 / 132. Page 13-14 / 133. Page 12 / 134. Page 33-34 / 135. Page 10 / 137. Page 86-87-88 / 138. Page 86-87 / 139. Page 88-89 / 140. Page 89-90 / 141. Page 59-60 / 142. Page 8 / 142. Page 8 / 143. Page 8 / 144. Page 9 / 145. Page 10 / 146. Page 10/ 147. Page 29-302 / 148. Page 30-31 / 149. Page 37-38 / 150. Page 91-92 /

ABOUT THE AUHTOR

I have been an inventory and financial specialist for twenty-five-plus years for national and international companies. Six years before becoming an inventory specialist and top store manager for numerous of regions and states, I wanted to become an assistant manager, store manager, regional trainer, district manager, and inventory specialist. To accomplish these above goals, I would work my ten hours a day shifts weekly within the company and try when I could between my duties to take notes, train on the job, and seek advice from other superior managers in my store on how to work and execute all departments within the store in order to get promotions within the company. I quickly realized most companies do not have enough tools and training hours to give most of their employees who want to be promoted within the company. They don't have a training program that will specifically train their employees and managers with patients on how to master, execute, and exceed inventory, financial numbers, their position as managers, to exceed and execute all company goals, exceed payroll, exceed systems controls, exceed and execute operations, production, and keep a great team. The amount of revenue (money) it takes to train employees is a lot of the reason why many companies and businesses will not invest in this type of training for their employees. This is why I invested in myself and others to achieve the goal in mastering inventory within any company in easy form.

If companies and businesses would invest in this type of training program, they would have even greater profit margins and increasing revenue throughout each year (increasing record-breaking numbers). Most companies hire their employees and managers then they train them for four days or two weeks on the job they were hired to do only. Most companies also give their employees different tests on chemical and health department rules, ServSafe, manager's daily task, and the employee's daily job functions during their training process. These types of training from companies are good, but it's not top execution training in controlling inventory to exceed company's profit margins. The majority of companies do not have a training class that will only teach their employees how to master and execute cost of goods, budgeting payroll schedules, financial information, food cost, hourly rate target, cash flow, budgeting monthly and quarterly reports, gauging gross profits, audits, auditor, operation profits, keeping numbers in line, state and federal requirements, and other critical matters that affect inventory and the company's profit. If companies had this type of training program, there would be more companies performing at top level success each year. Most companies and businesses will inform their employees and managers of the company's budget goals and sales goals each month and for the year, but companies don't teach their employees and managers how to reach and exceed these budget goals and sales goals.

All the above I had to master on my own time within six years with little help from coworkers and managers who didn't have time to train me and focus on their own daily job task. I worked each day on the job, looking, learning, studying, and training for all positions and departments within the company. I spent countless hours after work in my home reviewing and mastering inventory and budgets for companies, such as retail stores, fast-food chains, restaurants, production plants, hotels, and etc. My goal was accomplished in 1991. I then became instantly a company trainer, four months later I became an assistant manager, five months later I became a store manager. One year later I became a regional manager, two years later I became an inventory specialist for multicompanies in different cities and states, such as Alabama, Florida, Mississippi, Atlanta, New Orleans, and throughout the southeastern region. During my twenty-five-plus years of working with multiple companies, I have increased the revenue of many national and international companies and increased company's bottom line profit at 41 percent and more each year. I accomplished and exceeded in building and restoring many companies by tracking and executing their inventory and by training and working with employees and managers. I trained many management teams on how to put a profitable inventory action plan together that will show increasing results in sales and revenue within six weeks; this includes improving the company's inventory counts, tracking inventory, ordering, building inventory, building a profitable team, troubleshooting, etc. I enjoyed using the tools in this book in training over 952 employees throughout the southeastern region to become top inventory managers, company trainers, district managers, regional manager, and most employees opened their own business. I am proud to say 96 percent of the employees' income has increased to over $45,000 yearly, up to six figure digits yearly. All the companies and employees that I have trained over the years are still growing today with great increasing sales, revenue, and profits.